BLUE

—

Hayley Edwards-Dujardin

PRESTEL

Munich · London · New York

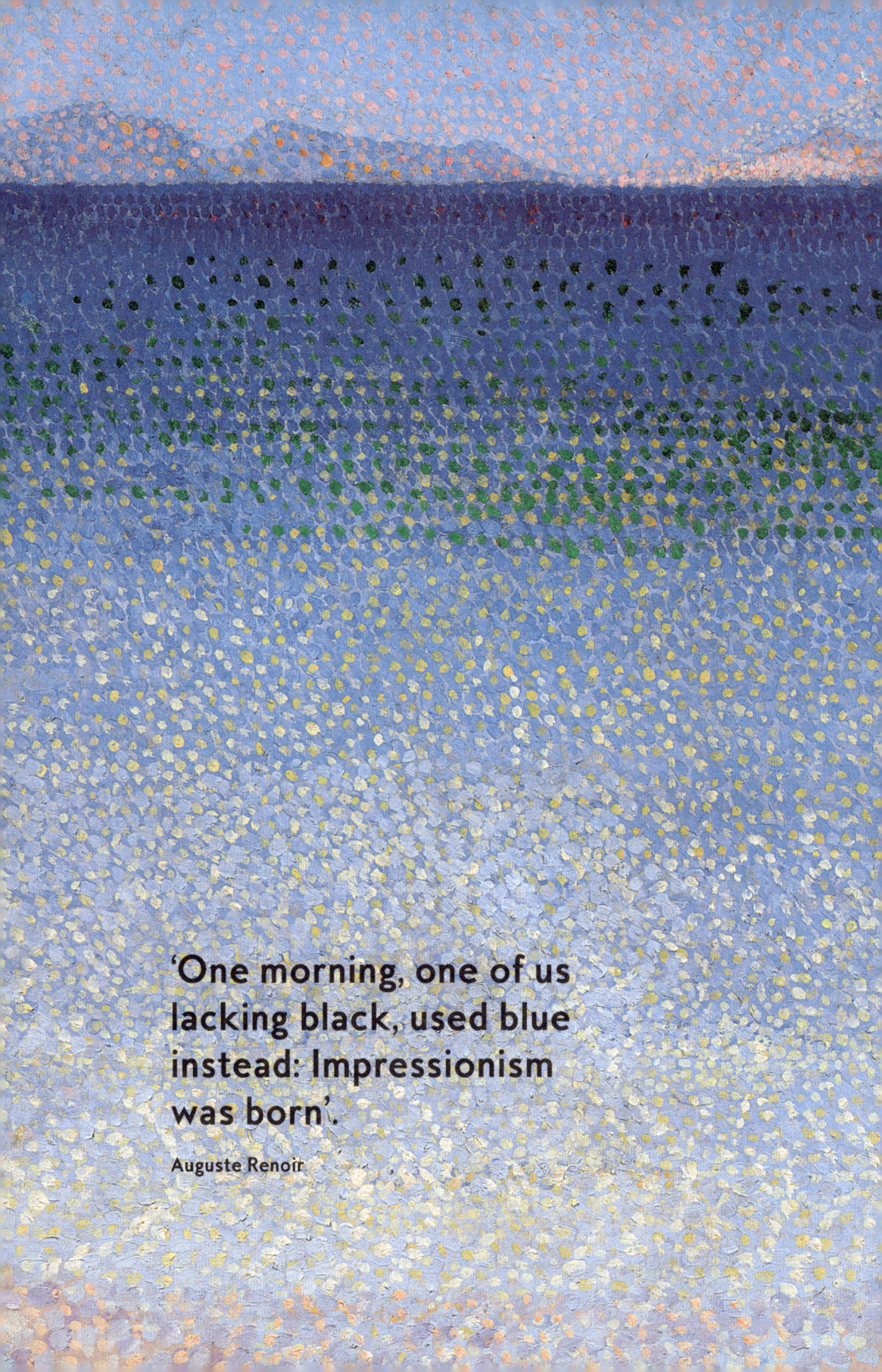

'One morning, one of us
lacking black, used blue
instead: Impressionism
was born'.

Auguste Renoir

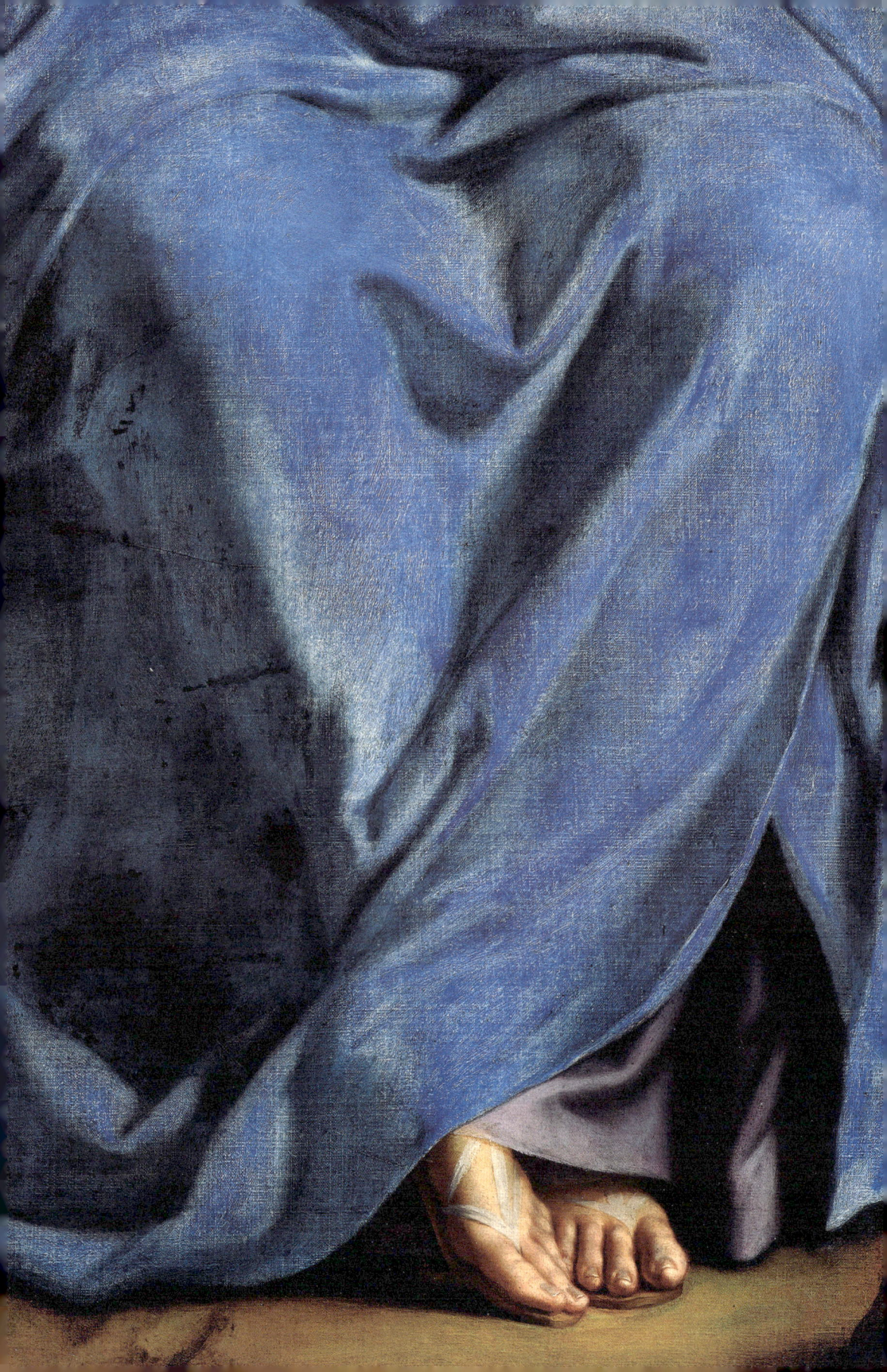

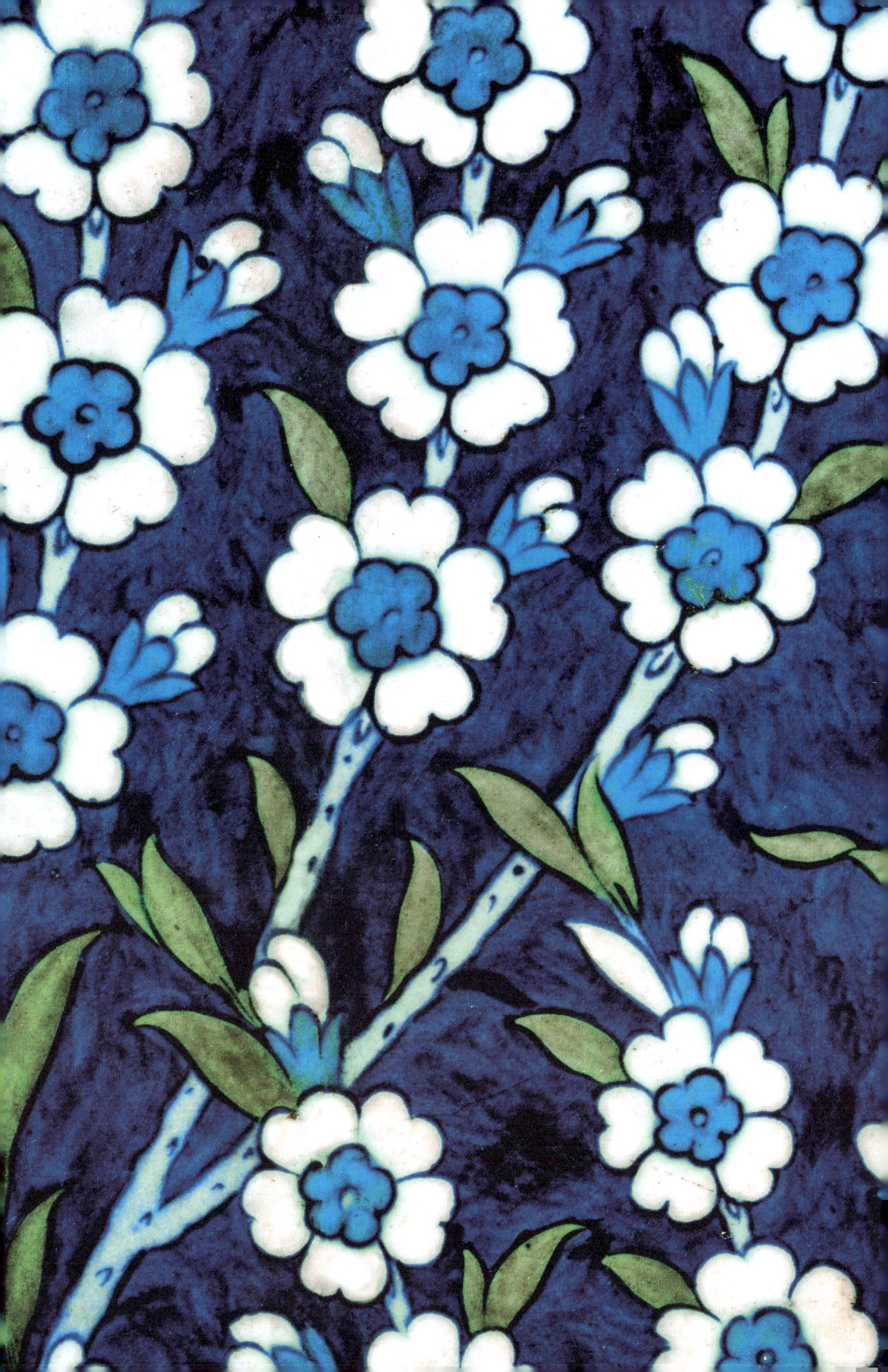

On Blue in Art

A Colour of Choice

What is so special about blue? Why does it so often achieve unanimity? Perhaps because it is terribly human in its contradictions. What other colour can boast that it is a symbol of hope and embodies sorrow, or proclaim itself a republican emblem whilst having a monarchical past?

Blue Down the Ages

To take an interest in blue is obviously to understand its place in art and above all to be aware that this colour, now so revered, took its time to triumph. Only in the Middle Ages did it finally assert itself when it took on divine connotations and became the Marian attribute par excellence. Yet during antiquity it had its moments, notably in Egypt but very little in Rome, where it was associated with the barbarians.

The Quest for Pigments

No study of blue in art can be dissociated from the history of pigments. Until the 19th century and the invention of chemical pigments, if one wanted to include blue in one's creations one had to be able to afford it. Only the Egyptians overcame this impediment by creating the first synthetic blue pigment in history, but their formula never spread further afield.
So elsewhere one had to rely on minerals such as lapis lazuli and plants such as indigo and woad.
Blue had its price.

There were of course other solutions but of lesser quality. Blue became a luxury commodity, and in the Middle Ages and the Renaissance it was used only in prestigious works on religious subjects.

✿ Natural Plant Pigments
▮ Natural Mineral Pigments
⚱ Synthetic Pigments

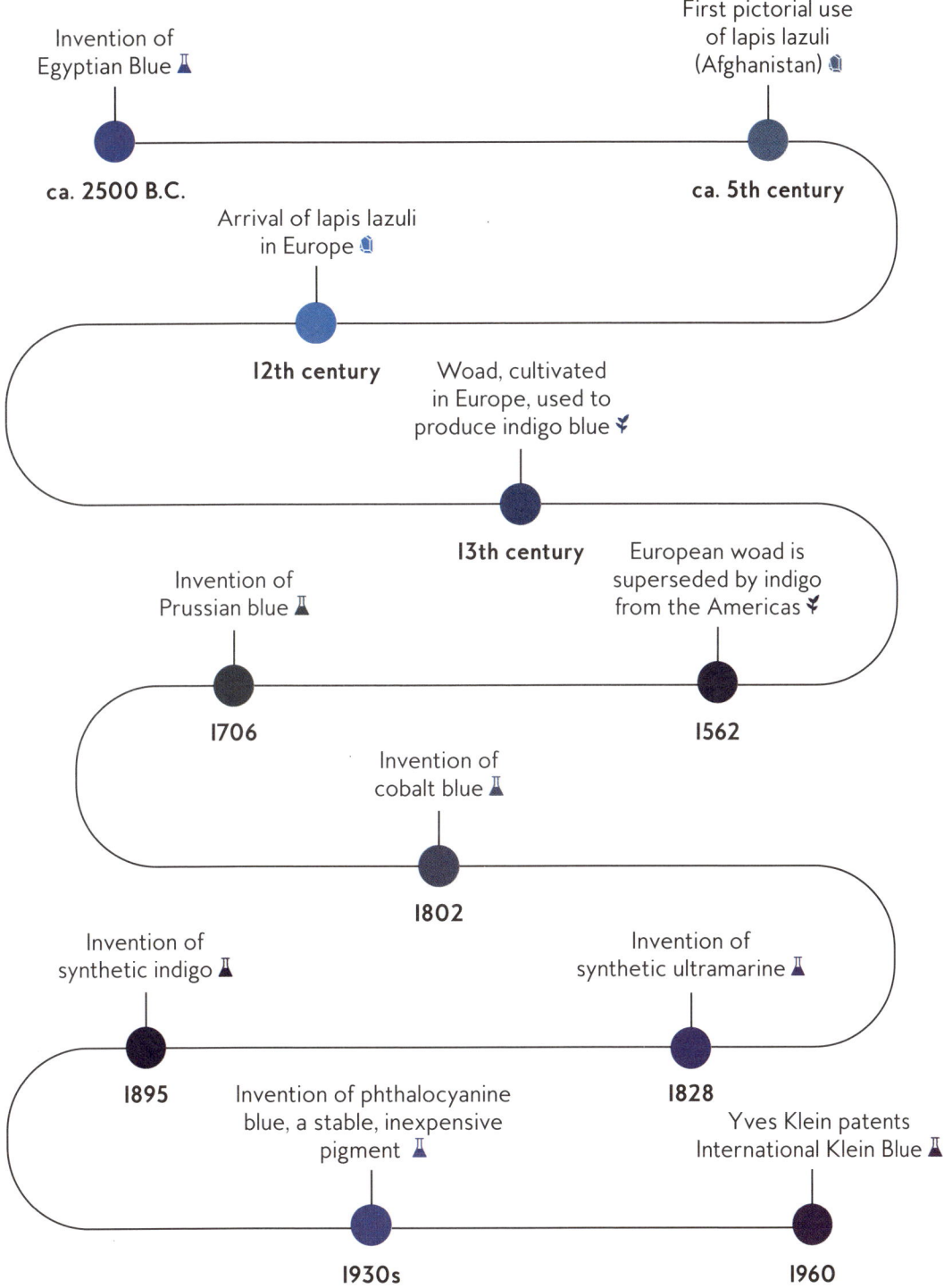

Invention of
Egyptian Blue ⚗

First pictorial use
of lapis lazuli
(Afghanistan) 💎

ca. 2500 B.C.

ca. 5th century

Arrival of lapis lazuli
in Europe 💎

12th century

Woad, cultivated
in Europe, used to
produce indigo blue ❦

13th century

European woad is
superseded by indigo
from the Americas ❦

Invention of
Prussian blue ⚗

1706

1562

Invention of
cobalt blue ⚗

1802

Invention of
synthetic indigo ⚗

Invention of
synthetic ultramarine ⚗

1895

1828

Invention of phthalocyanine
blue, a stable, inexpensive
pigment ⚗

Yves Klein patents
International Klein Blue ⚗

1930s

1960

'Black A, white E, red I, green U, blue O: you vowels ...,
O great trumpet blaring strange and piercing cries
Through silences where worlds and angels pass crosswise;
Omega, O, the violet brilliance of those eyes!'

Arthur Rimbaud, *Voyelles*, Poems, 1871

Hot and Cold

In his *Theory of Colours* (1810) Goethe classified blue as a warm colour and yellow as a cool colour. In absolute terms, there is no such categorisation since conventions vary. In the Middle Ages and the Renaissance blue was regarded as a warm colour but in ancient China it was female and cold.

The Secret of Blue

In Poésies, Jean Cocteau gave us the secret of blue: 'In Naples, the Virgin stays in the cracks in the walls when the sky recedes. But it's all a mystery. The mystery of sapphire, mystery of Sainte-Vierge, mystery of the siphon, mystery of the sailor's collar, mystery of the blue rays that blind and your blue eye that goes through my heart'.

Towards a Freer Use

When production of synthetic pigments proliferated, blue became widely available and artists could use it at will. It triumphed in grandiose skies in landscape paintings, seascapes and shimmering fabrics because in art blue is the great ally of light.

It was above all when artists began using it as they pleased that blue ceased to be the sole preserve of the sea and sky. Beginning in the late 19th century they dared to paint faces and bodies and even animals and urban buildings in blue. A realist colour became a reflection of emotions.

Life in Blue

In the 20th century blue played a prominent role in the development of certain artists. For Picasso it was a refuge during a difficult period of his life; for the founders of the Blue Rider group (p. 46), Franz Marc and Wassily Kandinsky, it became the symbol of a revolutionary artistic movement; and Yves Klein went as far as to name his emblematic blue after himself.

Blue became indispensable, whether given naturalistic, decorative or sentimental connotations. It became so essential that when 19th-century researchers noted that blue was almost completely absent in the art of the ancient Greeks they erroneously concluded that there could only be one reason for this: the Greeks must have been afflicted by a visual deficiency preventing them from seeing this colour, for who would not want to paint blue?

Lapis lazuli from Afghanistan
Polished slab containing pyrite
Natural History Museum, London

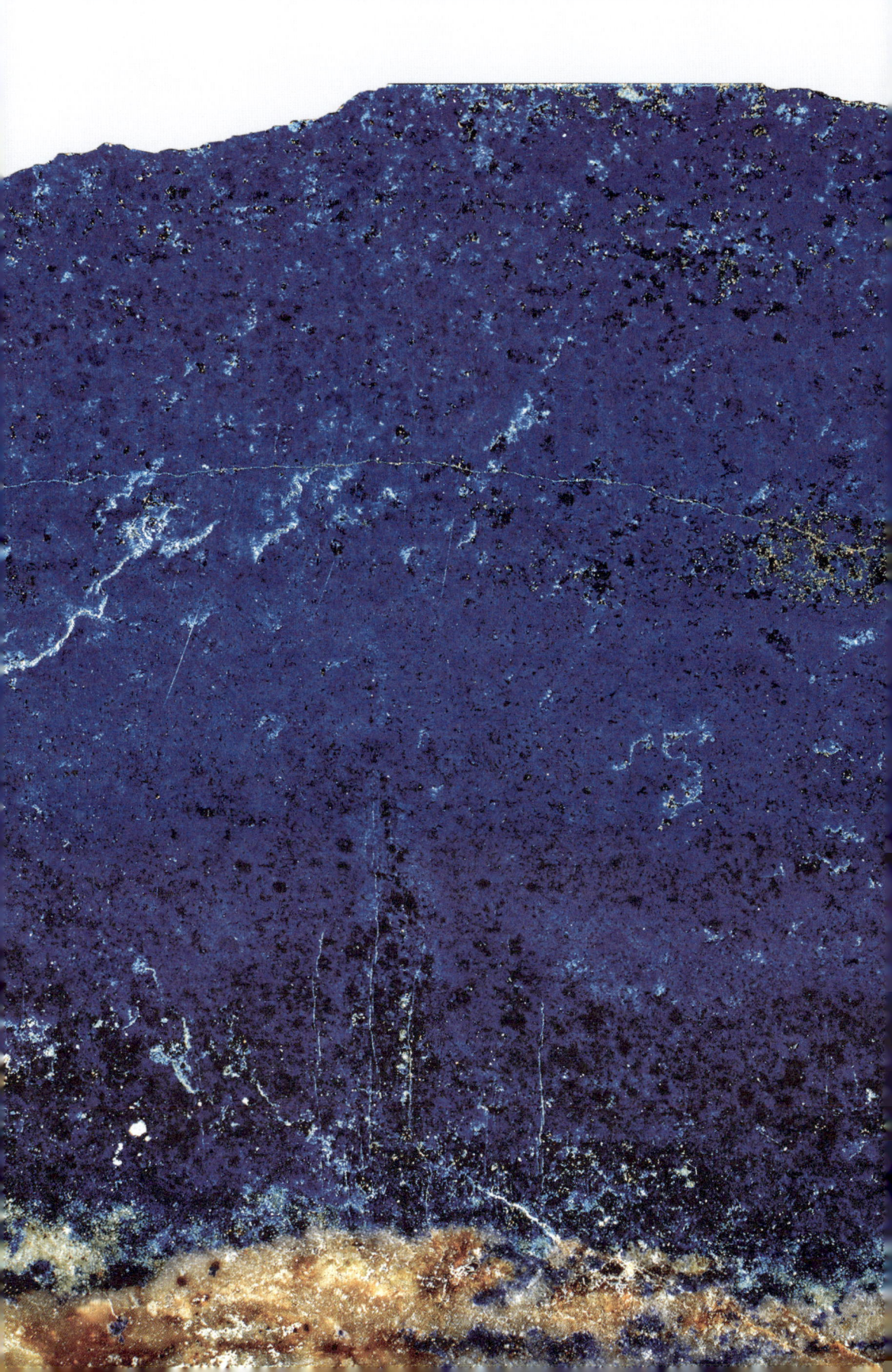

Geography

Sources of the Principal Pigments

Natural Plant Pigments

 Indigo:
Africa, India and
South America

 Pastel or woad:
Northern England
and France (Alsace,
Normandy, Languedoc)

Natural Mineral Pigments

 Lapis lazuli:
Afghanistan (historically),
today mined worldwide

 Azurite:
Hungary (historically)
then Namibia, Arizona and
France (Chessy in the 19th
century), now almost
everywhere

Synthetic Pigments

 Egyptian blue:
Egypt

 Ultramarine:
France

 Cobalt blue:
France

 Indigo:
Germany

 Prussian blue:
Germany

A Priceless Ore

Most of the lapis lazuli used to produce ultramarine in the West before the eighteenth century came from the mines at Sar-e Sang in Afghanistan. In 1271 Marco Polo discovered this 'high mountain from which one extracts the most beautiful blue'.

A Colour Index

From Pigment to Tube

In the beginning there is a pigment, either natural (vegetable or mineral) or synthetic (produced chemically).
But naming a colour after its pigment of origin can often prove complex. For example, what would you associate ferrocyanide with? Probably not Prussian blue. Yet that is what it is. To avoid confusion, colour manufacturers refer to the Colour Index International, a reference database in which Prussian blue is listed as PB27. A pigment has to be mixed with a binder (wax, resin, oil, etc.) and various additives to finally become a paint ready to use.

Naming Colours

'Ultramarine', historically obtained from lapis lazuli, denotes nuances of deep, violet-tinted blue. In colour charts it can have a variety of often fanciful names ranging from 'Guimet Blue' (Guimet invented synthetic ultramarine) to 'Giotto Blue', 'Faience Blue' and 'Poet Blue'. And of course there is Yves Klein's famous International Klein Blue, a derivative of ultramarine.

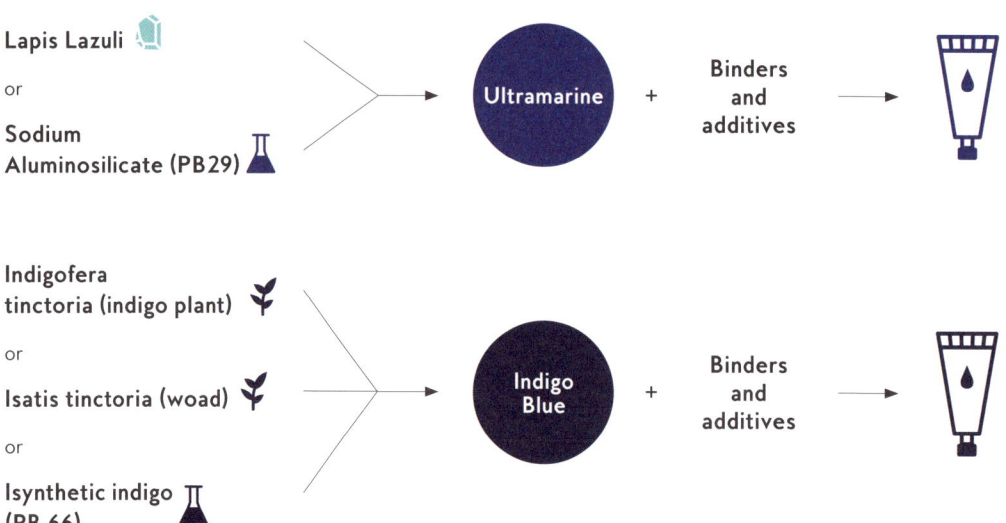

Lapis Lazuli

or

Sodium Aluminosilicate (PB29)

Ultramarine + Binders and additives

Indigofera tinctoria (indigo plant)

or

Isatis tinctoria (woad)

or

Isynthetic indigo (PB 66)

Indigo Blue + Binders and additives

PB 15
Phtalo blue

PB 27
Prussian blue
> *The Great Wave Off Kanagawa (p. 35)*

PB 28
Cobalt blue
> *The Starry Night (p. 37)*
> *The Golden Cell (p. 83)*

PB 29
Ultramarine
> *The Very Rich Hours of the Duke of Berry (p. 25)*
> *Woman Reading a Letter (p. 31)*

PB 30
Azure

PB 31
Egyptian blue
> *Sphinx of Amenhotep III (p. 17)*
> *Diana (p. 65)*

PB 32
Smalt

PB 33
Manganese blue

PB 35
Cerulean blue

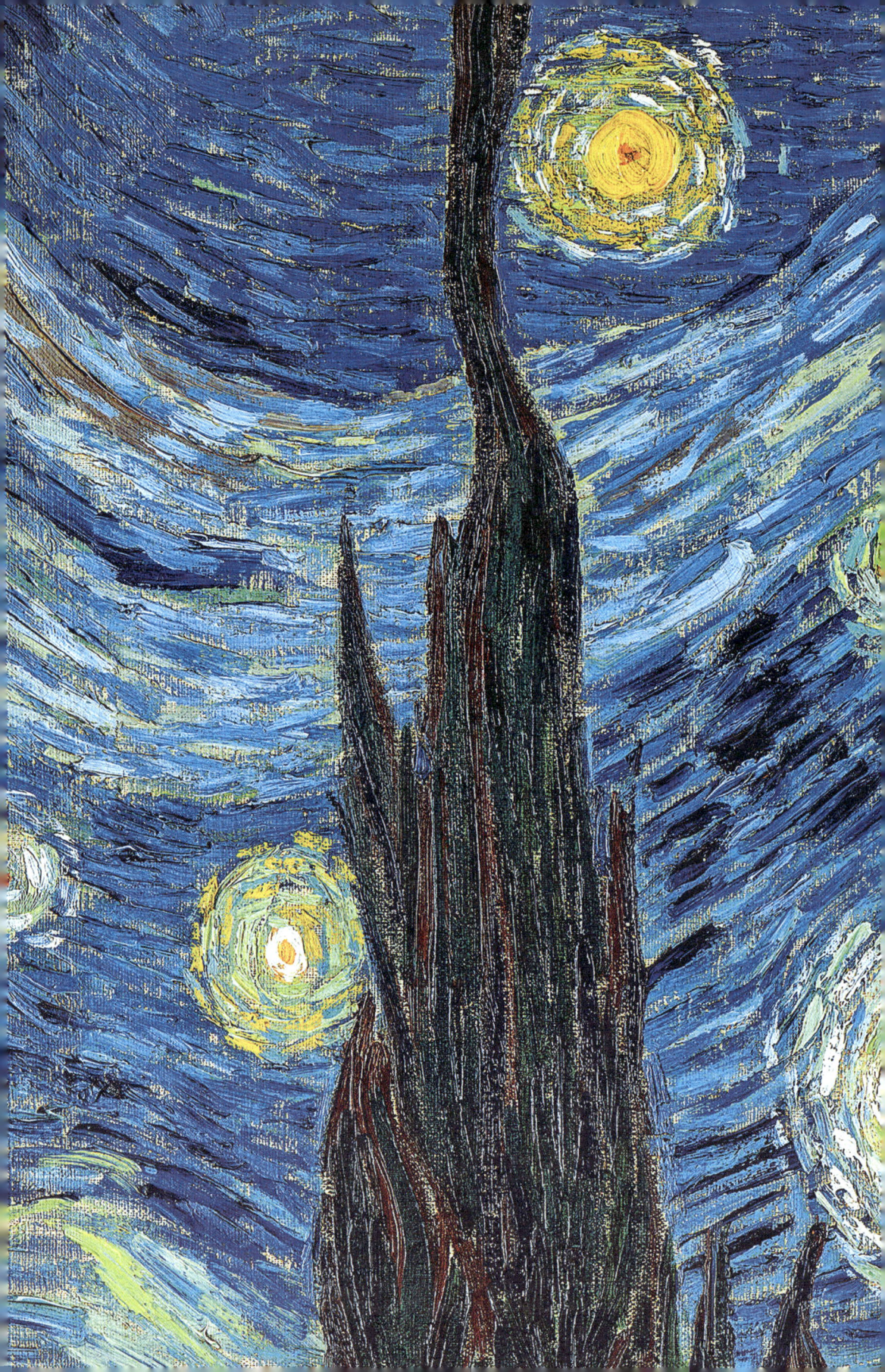

THE ESSENTIALS

—

Sphinx of Amenhotep III

ca. 1390–52 B.C.

The Production of Egyptian Blue

It is produced from a mixture of silica, lime, copper and an alkali (its colour is due to a calcium-copper tetrasilicate), fired at a temperature between 870 and 1100 °C. This produces a blue glass paste which is ground into a fine powder to be used as a pigment.

The Secret of Production

Egyptian artists usually passed on their knowledge orally, as attested by the inscription on the stele of the painter Irtysen, ca. 2030 B.C.: 'I know how to make pigments and substances which melt without fire burning them and are also insoluble in water. I will reveal this to no one except my eldest son, God having ordained that he practice as an initiate …'

An Eternal Blue

In Ancient Egypt the production of coloured earthenware reached its peak during the reign of the pharaoh Amenhotep III. It was called tjehnet ('scintillating'), like the pharaoh, who was also known by this epithet. Valuable gifts and funerary and religious objects were produced with this brilliant finish.

This small sphinx is engraved with the pharaoh's name. The face's stylised features evoke the monarch who instead of lion's paws has arms and hands bearing offerings. This figurine is both a representation of Amenhotep III and an object for his probable worship, even after death, in a temple built in his honour.

Its brilliant blue glaze was neither rare nor merely decorative. This colour was prized by the Egyptians, for whom it symbolised the sky, water and above all creation, rebirth and holiness. The fact that figurines like this have been found in tombs also indicates that they probably played a role as talismans, due to their subject – the powerful and protective sphinx/pharaoh – but also due to their celestial colour warding off evil spirits.

The Egyptians were the first to create an artificial blue pigment, Egyptian blue, around 2500 B.C. The secret of its production was rediscovered in the 19th century, when it was renamed Pompeian blue, probably because it was thought this more evocatively suggested fantasies of a buried past.

Sphinx of Amenhotep III
ca. 1390–52 BC
Glazed earthenware
The Metropolitan Museum of Art, New York

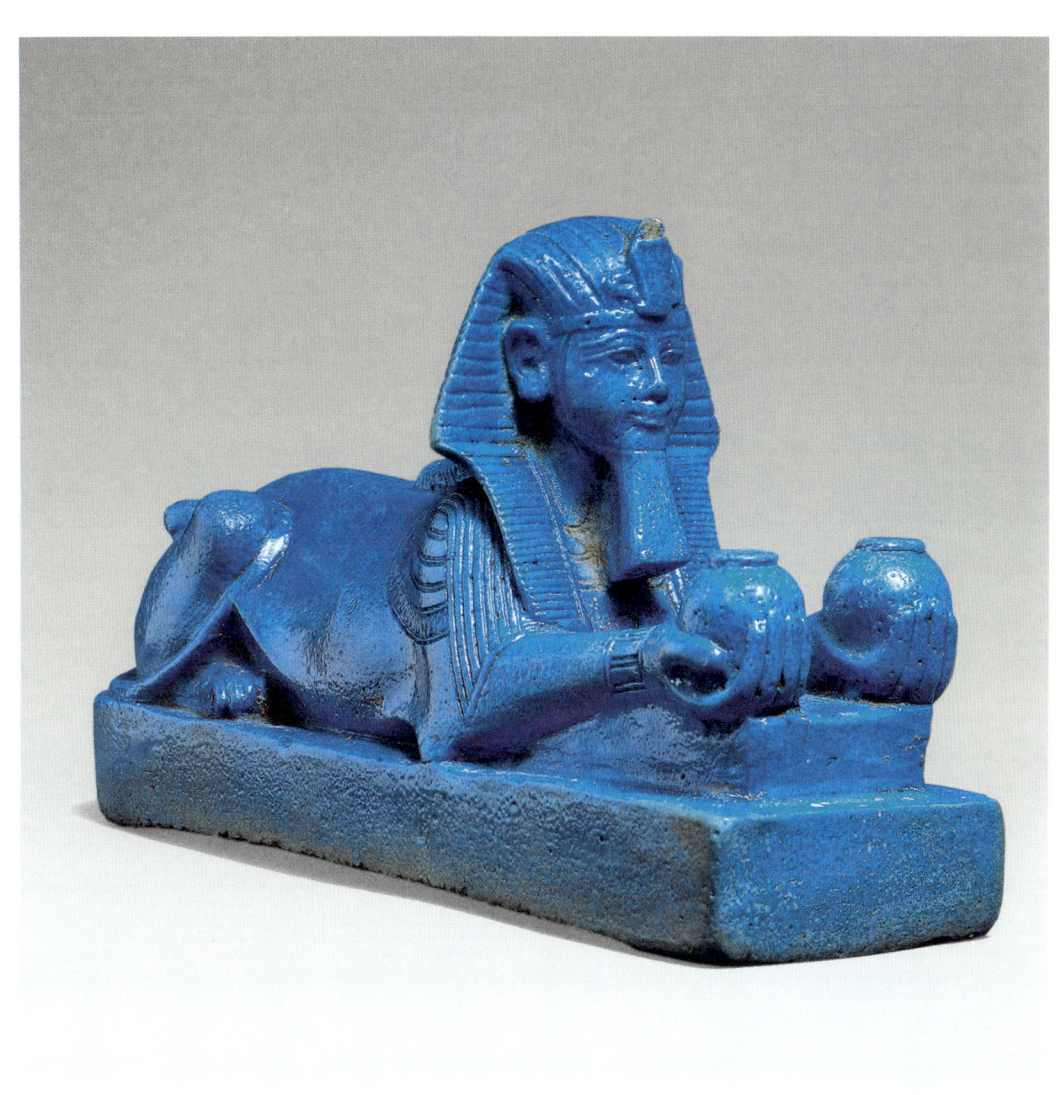

'I preside in the heavens like a misunderstood sphinx'.

Charles Baudelaire, 'La Beauté', *Les Fleurs du mal*

Joachim's Dream

1303-5

The Artist's Trick

Ultramarine can be used on damp plaster but would have been too expensive for an entire chapel. So to obtain such a deep blue on some walls Giotto abandoned the fresco technique - requiring the plaster to be still damp - and used azurite pigments on dry plaster. A trick that went unnoticed.

From Giotto to Twombly

In 2010 the Louvre inaugurated a new ceiling painted by Cy Twombly. A series of spheres float peripherally around a blue sky, a blue that the artist describes as being 'not the blue of Greece, or the sky or the sea. It was the blue of painting, Giotto's Blue that I wanted, a simple, full blue between cobalt and lapis lazuli'.

An Infinite Blue

At the beginning of the 14th century the merchant Enrico Scrovegni decided to extend his palace in the centre of the city of Padua by building a family chapel dedicated to his father.

The chapel's walls and vault are entirely painted with frescoes depicting thirty-six episodes from the Old and New Testaments and grisailles representing the Vices and Virtues. All were painted by the Florentine artist Giotto. Considered his most remarkable work, the Scrovegni Chapel became a model for the art of the Trecento.

In his frescoes Giotto imposes a narrative language in which he treats a scene's principal subjects and its secondary, anecdotal figures with the same rigour, thereby abolishing the habitual distinctions between heavenly and earthly, the prodigious and the mundane.

A unifying element is his use of blue, a deep blue symbolising the starry firmament in the chapel's vaults and serving as a celestial backdrop for various biblical episodes on the walls. Ultramarine, valued as much for its mysticism as for the preciousness of this pigment produced from lapis lazuli imported from the Orient, encourages us to lose ourselves in the infinite.

This is a detail from Giotto's depiction of Joachim's Dream, the passage in the Bible in which an angel announces to Joachim that his infertile wife, Anne, will give birth to a child, Mary, who in turn will become the mother of the Son of God. The theme accentuates the work's dreamlike atmosphere. The angel's intensified movement stands out strikingly against the penetrating blue sky, acting as the link between the spiritual and temporal.

'… where the entire vault and the background of the frescoes are so blue that it seems that the radiant day has also crossed the threshold with the visitor'.

Marcel Proust's description of the blue in the Scrovegni Chapel

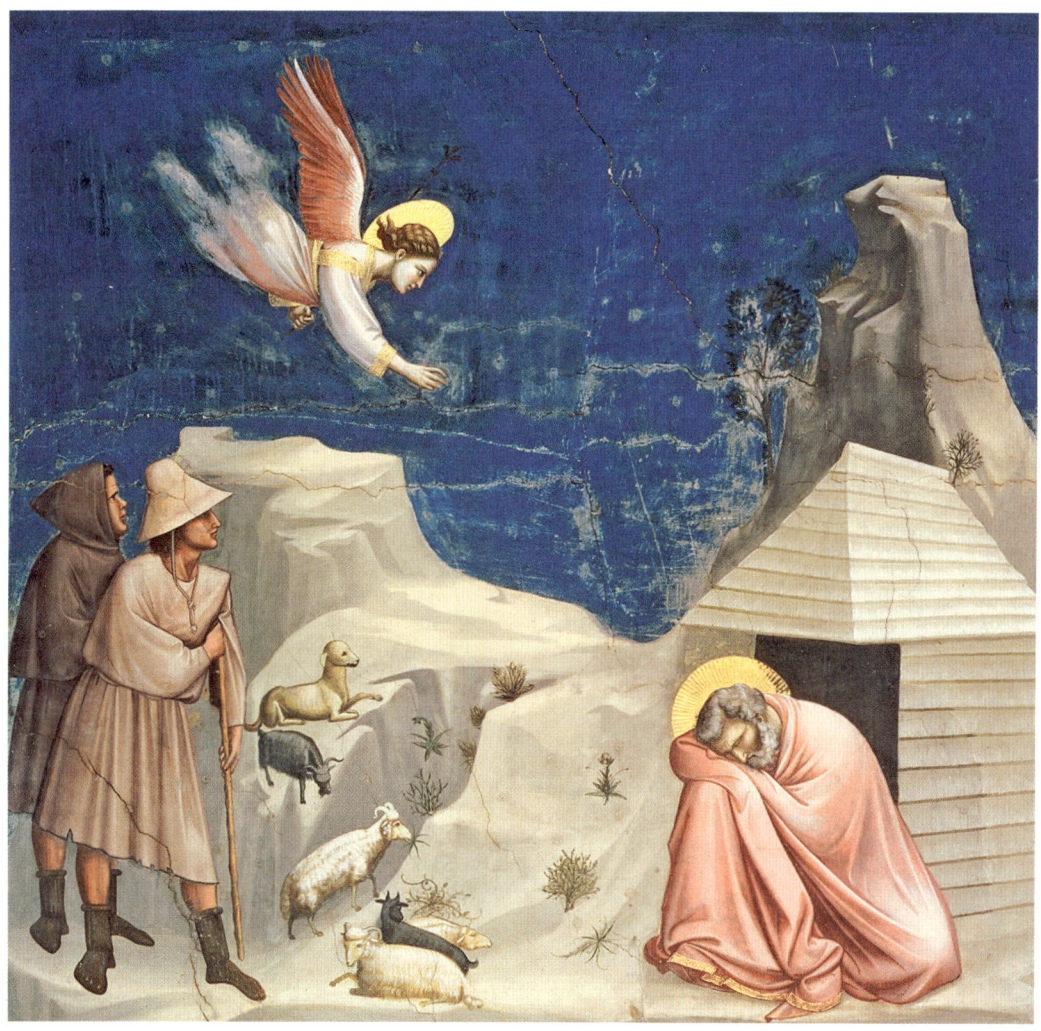

Joachim's Dream
Giotto (1267–1337)
1303–5
Fresco
Scrovegni Chapel, Padua

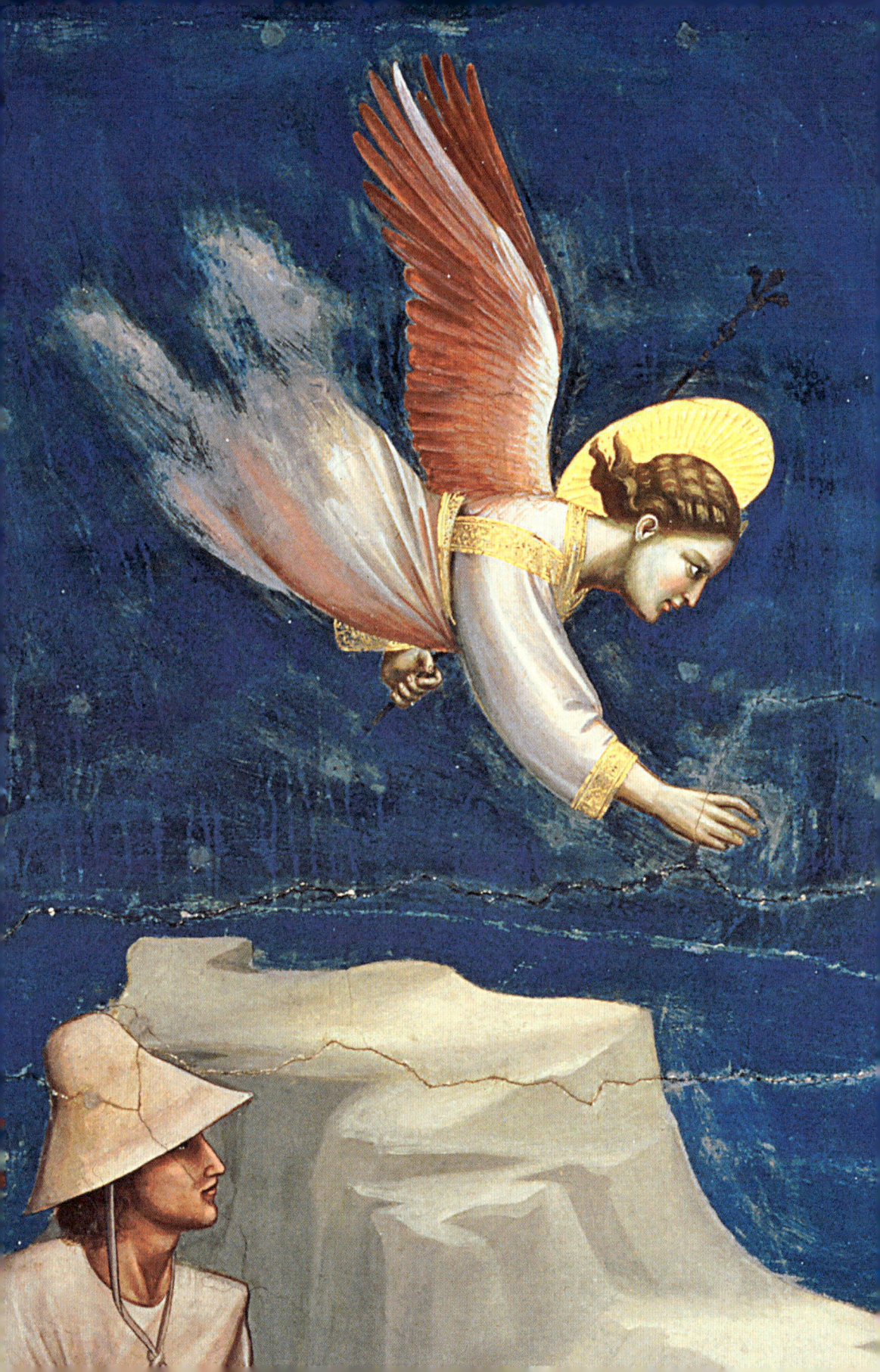

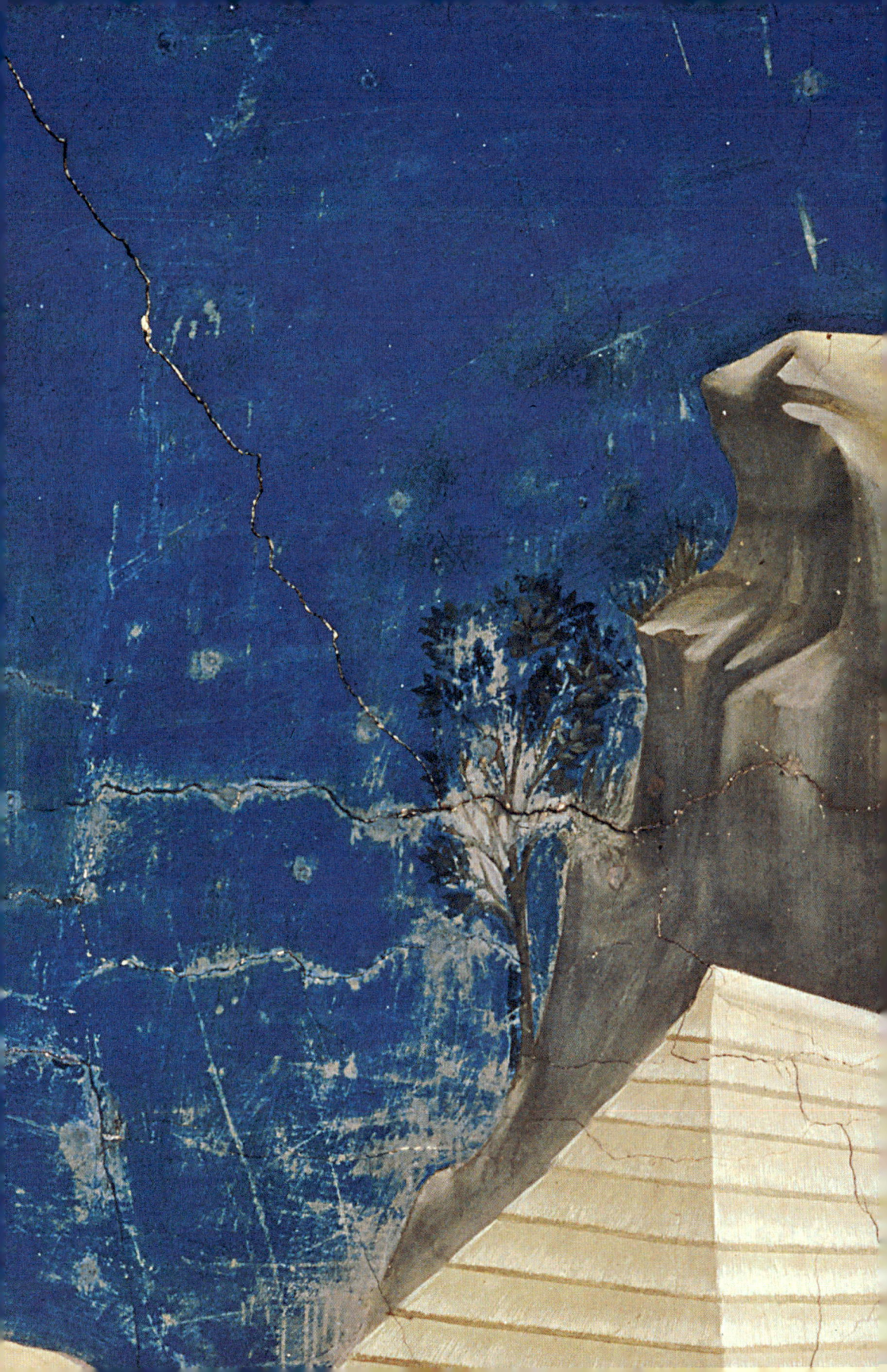

Meiping vase

ca. 1350

GUIDELINES

The 'blue and white'

Yuan period (1279–1368)	appearance of 'blue and white' ceramics
Export to the Middle East	14th century
15th century	Influence on Iranian pottery
Golden age of 'blue and white'	**Ming period** (1368–1644)
16th century	Export to Europe
Cobalt blue and the perfection of exuberance	**Qing period** (1644–1912)

A Symbolic Alliance

The Yuan, the Mongol dynasty that reigned over China from 1279 to 1368, encouraged the development of ceramics and particularly the so-called 'blue and white' porcelain.

The import of cobalt by sea via the Persian Gulf enabled the artisans of the Yuan dynasty to produce new pieces with blue and white decoration, but only because cobalt is one of the very few pigments, with copper oxide red and iron oxide red, that can withstand the high temperatures required to fire porcelain.

The first blue and white pieces produced during the Yuan period are small and have dark blue decoration painted on a white ground. As this technique was perfected, artisans began producing monumental pieces with intense blue grounds like this Meiping vase, used to display branches of plum blossom. The sinuous body of the intricately detailed white dragon contrasts with the corpulence of the vase and the fullness of the cobalt blue.

The combination of blue and white also had a symbolic meaning for the Mongols, a people believed to have originated from the union of a blue wolf and a white deer. This type of ceramics thus embodied the link between belief and regalia.

Meiping vase with dragon decoration
ca. 1350
Porcelain
Musée Guimet, Paris

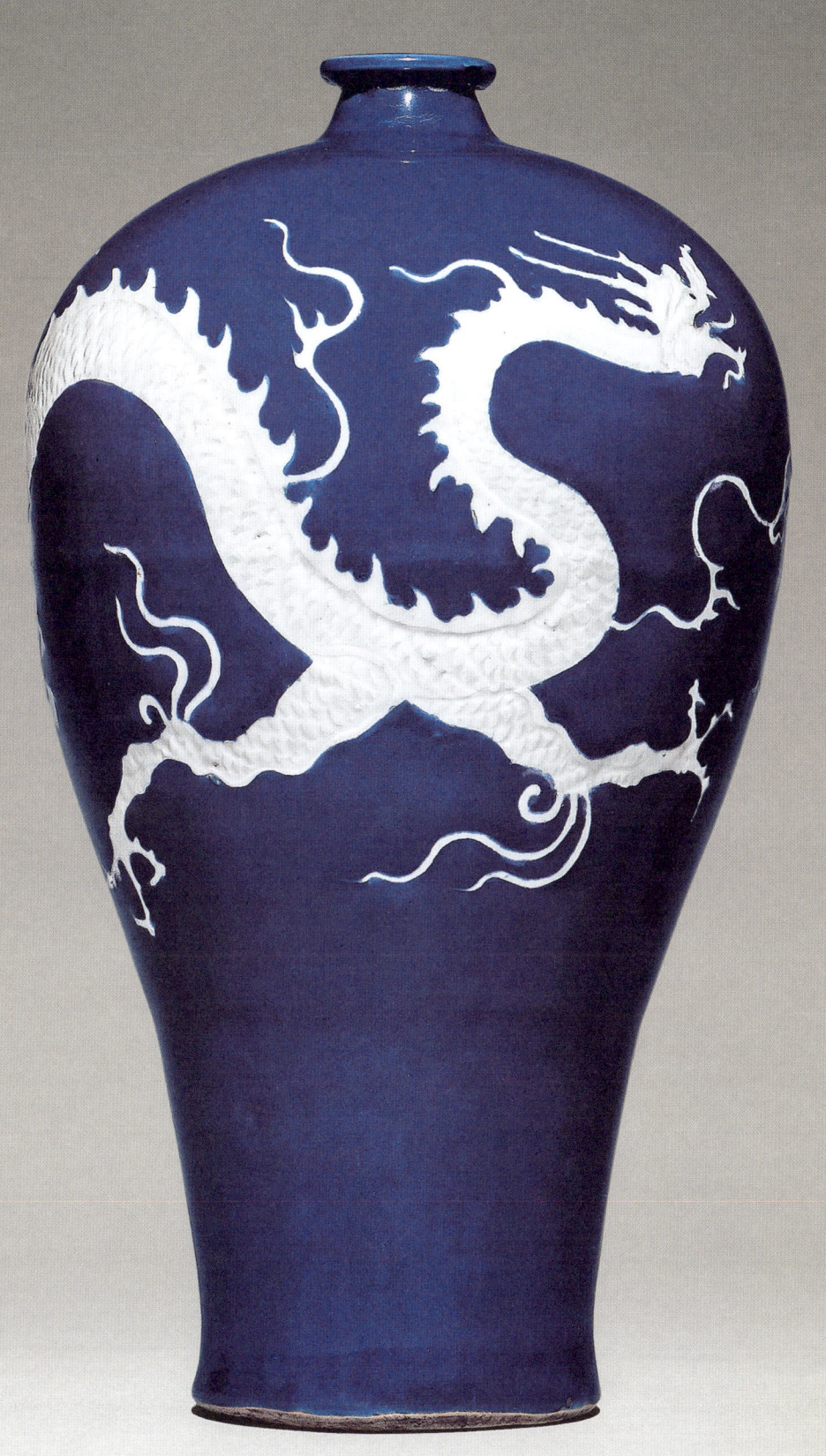

The Very Rich Hours of the Duke of Berry

1416

Stars and Horoscopes

In the 12th century the knowledge of astronomy and astrology (then regarded as one) developed in the Arab world and spread to Europe. These disciplines were taught in universities and were in favour with popes and kings. When astrology began to flourish during the Renaissance every royal court had its astrologer, Queen Elisabeth I her John Dee and Catherine de Médicis her Nostradamus.

TIMELINE
Famous Books of Hours

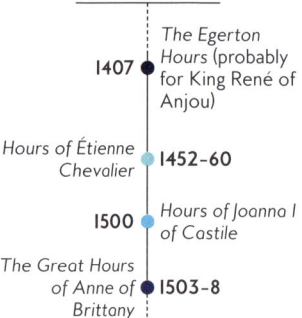

1407 — *The Egerton Hours* (probably for King René of Anjou)

Hours of Étienne Chevalier — **1452–60**

1500 — *Hours of Joanna I of Castile*

The Great Hours of Anne of Brittany — **1503–8**

The Very Rich Hours of the Duke of Berry
Calendar, folio 9, September
Limbourg brothers
1416
Musée Condé, Chantilly

The Pigments of the Zodiac

In the Middle Ages Catholics possessed liturgical books called 'books of hours', composed of prayers appropriate to the different times of day. They included psalms and a calendar, and the most sophisticated versions were richly illustrated.

Around 1410 the Duke of Berry commissioned the three Limbourg brothers, painters, to create a book of hours. This manuscript is exceptional in that, in addition to its calligraphed texts with ornately decorated margins, it contains nearly a hundred exquisite miniatures.

The most famous images of the *Very Rich Hours of the Duke of Berry* are those illustrating its calendar. Thanks to the wealth of their patron, the artists working on the manuscript could use luxurious pigments such a lapis lazuli for the blues, vermilion red and pink lacquer. These brilliant colours enhance each scene's precise description, further heightened by the artists' dexterity and a use of perspective rivalling that of Italian artists.

The miniature shown here, representing the month of September, depicts a grape harvesting scene in front of the Château de Saumur. The luminous blue sky dominating the landscape extends above into a hemicycle containing detailed astrological gradations. Illustrated are the zodiac signs of the month in question, Virgo and Libra, above the god Apollo in his chariot, associated with the sun. The sky was a pretext for such a sumptuous use of blue, but it goes without saying that it was also a way to epitomise the wealth and splendour of the artists' many successive patrons. Unfinished after the deaths of the Limbourg brothers and the Duke of Berry in 1416, this book of hours was completed by Jean Colombe for the Duke of Savoie around 1485.

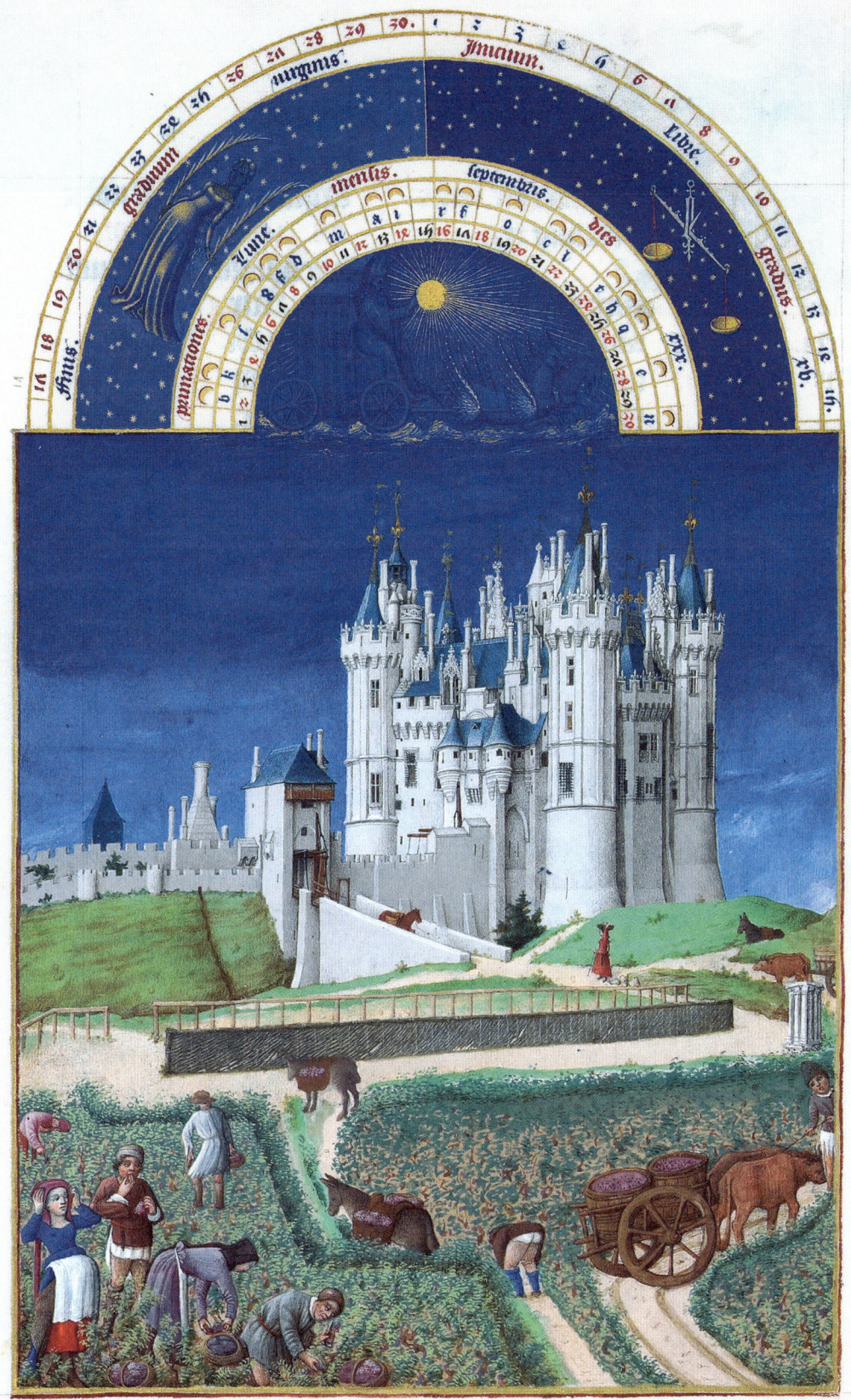

The Coronation of Louis VIII and Blanche of Castile in 1223

1460

Regalia

This term denotes the symbolic objects used during the coronation ceremonies of the kings of France. Most of the regalia - at least those still in existence - are now in the Louvre and Saint-Denis Abbey, including Joyeuse, the sword said to be Charlemagne's, Charles V's sceptre and Louis XV's crown.

The Symbols of Royalty

Crown: sovereignty
Sceptre: political power
Hand of justice: justice
Sword: military power
Spurs: chivalry
Fleur-de-lys-patterned mantle: hereditary divine power

Sacrebleu

In 1250 Saint Louis asked Primat, a monk in Saint-Denis Abbey, to write a chronicle of the French monarchy. Titled *Le Roman des rois* (Romance of Kings), it was completed in 1274.

Other monks and ensuing French kings decided to continue Primat's work with additions to his manuscript, subsequently called *Grandes chroniques de France*. From Charles V's reign, this history of the kings of France became hugely popular, despite being primarily destined for princes and their entourages, for it is illustrated with exquisite miniatures and was therefore extremely costly.

In the mid-15th century the artist Jean Fouquet took on the task of illustrating the manuscript written from 1415 to 1420 and completed in 1455–60. Forced to adapt his work to the text, he could not choose the scenes he depicted - these chronicles were intended to glorify the nobles, in this case very probably Charles VII (even though the patron who commissioned it remains unknown). Many of his miniatures depict coronations and crusades.

Here Jean Fouquet is depicting the coronation of Louis VIII and his wife Blanche of Castile at Reims in 1223. A renowned court painter influenced by the Italian Renaissance, Fouquet was also a trained illuminator. He demonstrated his skill in detailed compositions conceived according to the Golden Section.

The omnipresence of blue in the image is not surprising. After its use in religious iconography, especially in Marian symbolism, it took on a political signification when the fleur-de-lis on a blue ground (the Capetians' coat of arms) became the emblem of the kings of France. From floor to ceiling, royalty is clothed in blue magnificence.

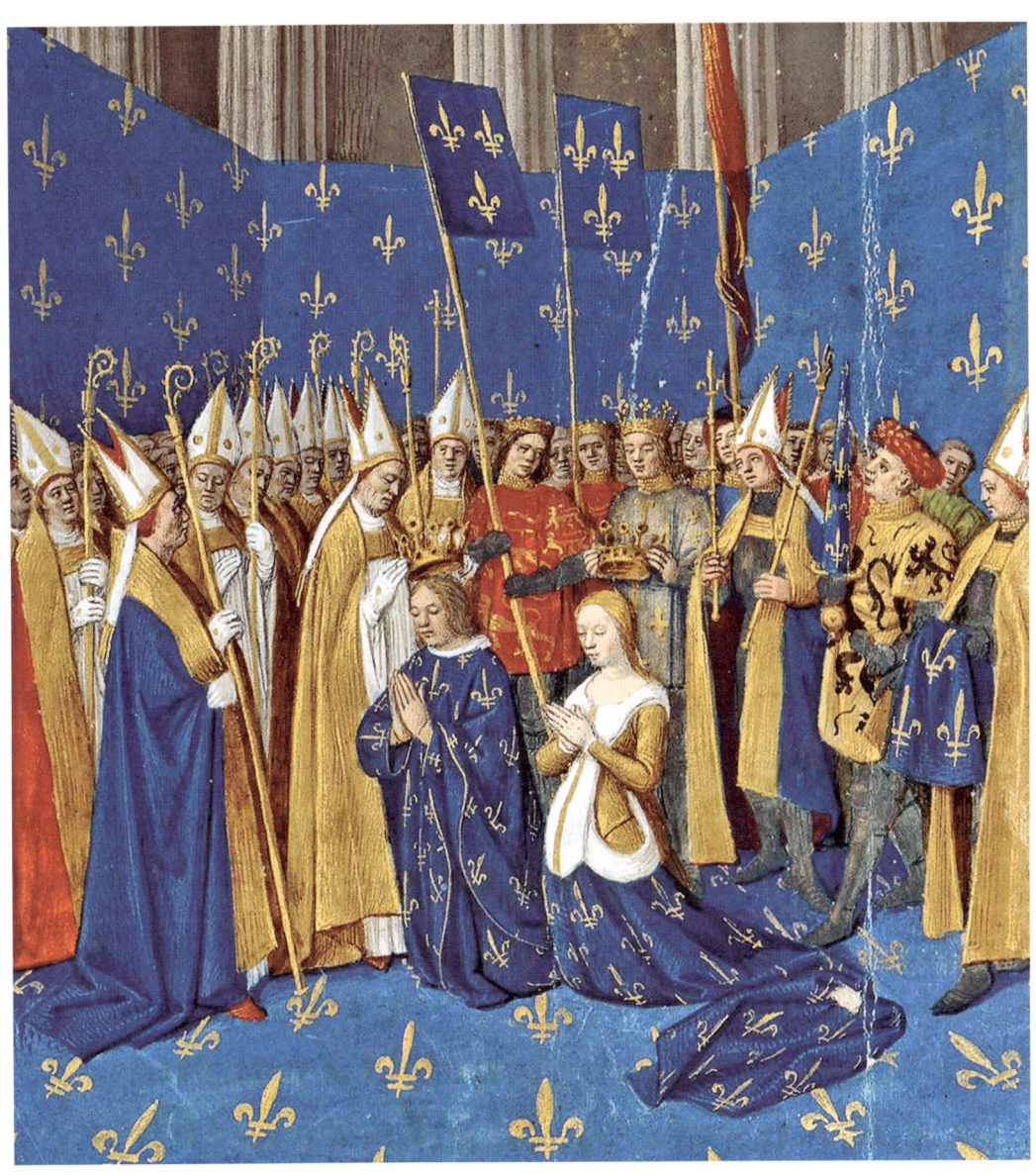

Coronation of Louis VIII
and Blanche de Castile in 1223
Illuminated manuscript, Saint-Denis Abbey
Jean Fouquet (1420–78/81)
1460
Bibliothèque nationale de France, Paris

Virgin of the Sorrows

1657

A modern legend

The use of lapis lazuli in the Middle Ages and the Renaissance was less widespread than believed, due to its prohibitive cost. More often than not, a similar blue pigment was produced from another mineral, azurite, less luminous but much more affordable.

TIMELINE
A Few Blue Virgins

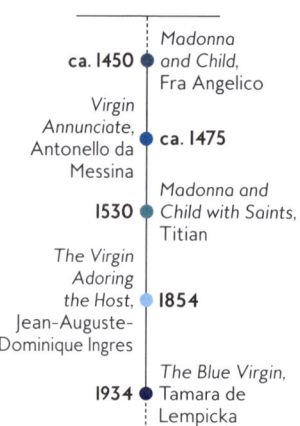

ca. 1450 ● *Madonna and Child,* Fra Angelico

Virgin Annunciate, Antonello da Messina ● ca. 1475

1530 ● *Madonna and Child with Saints,* Titian

The Virgin Adoring the Host, Jean-Auguste-Dominique Ingres ● 1854

1934 ● *The Blue Virgin,* Tamara de Lempicka

Virgin of the Sorrows
Philippe de Champaigne (1602–74)
1657
Oil on canvas
178 x 125 cm
Musée du Louvre, Paris

The Cost of the Divine

In traditional portrayals the Virgin Mary is often cloaked in a voluminous blue mantle. But the reason for this is less mystical than one might think.

Not until around the 15th century did Marian iconography become fully associated with blue. Before then the Virgin could be seen dressed in grey, brown or even black, because she was usually a symbol of a mother's suffering. And when artists sought to paint her in her sacred grandeur or accentuate her purity, they opted for red. So why blue? The allusion to the sky is obvious: the Virgin is an intermediary between the earthly and the heavenly.

But there could well be another, more pragmatic reason for this. The cult of the Virgin Mary was then in full expansion and patrons of religious works intent on paying a tribute to her befitting her glory were prepared to pay a high price. This price was the cost of the ultramarine blue obtained from lapis lazuli imported from Afghanistan. The use of this extremely expensive deep blue pigment and none other became a major contractual stipulation.

Because Philippe de Champaigne sought to portray a grief-stricken rather than grandiose Virgin Mary he chose a modest and melancholic blue. The painter is depicting a Virgin of Sorrows leaning against the Cross on which her son sacrificed himself. Even though he includes Christian symbolism – the crown of thorns and nails at the mother of Christ's feet and Jerusalem under a threateningly dark sky in the background – he portrays her in a moment of very human bereavement. With her hands resignedly crossed and her slightly slumped posture, this is a woman in despair. Only the dominant blue provides a note of heavenly hope in this vision of melancholy.

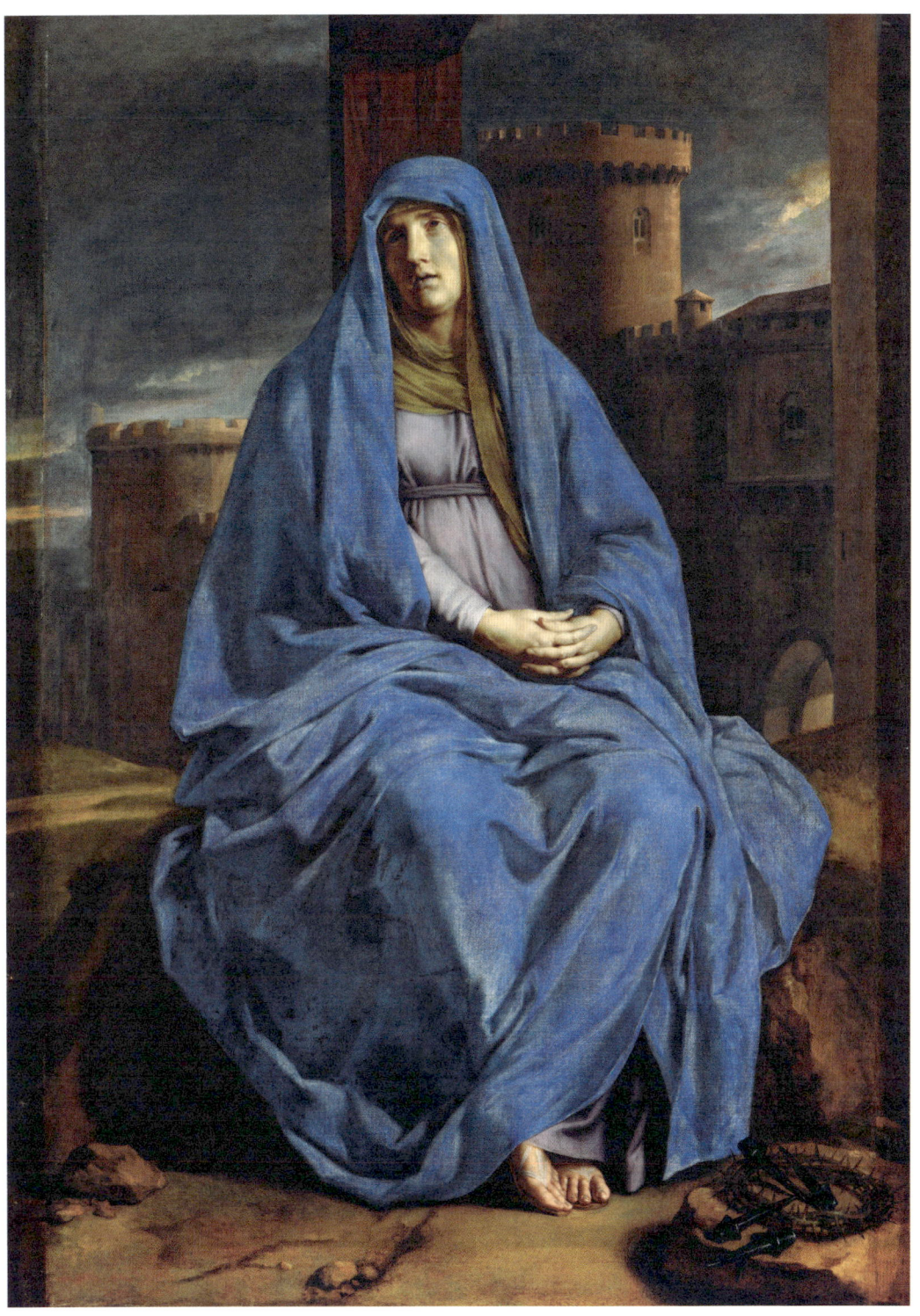

Woman Reading a Letter

1662/63

Description with Colour

In 1888 Van Gogh wrote to Émile Bernard: 'For instance, do you know a painter called Vermeer, who, for example, painted a very beautiful Dutch lady, pregnant? This strange painter's palette is blue, lemon yellow, pearl grey, black, white. Of course, in his few paintings there are, if it comes to it, all the riches of a complete palette, but the arrangement of lemon yellow, pale blue, pearl grey is as characteristic of him as that of black, white, grey and pink is of Velázquez'.

GUIDELINE
Women in Blue

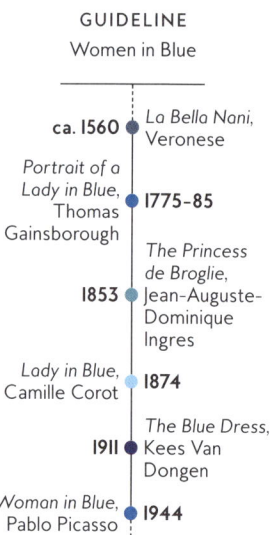

ca. 1560	*La Bella Nani,* Veronese
Portrait of a Lady in Blue, Thomas Gainsborough	1775–85
1853	*The Princess de Broglie,* Jean-Auguste-Dominique Ingres
Lady in Blue, Camille Corot	1874
1911	*The Blue Dress,* Kees Van Dongen
Woman in Blue, Pablo Picasso	1944

'I'll write to you'

To look at a picture by Vermeer is to imagine an entire world, an intimate, calm world admittedly, but that is what is so intriguing. What is going on in the lives of these people?

This picture depicts a young woman absorbed in reading a letter, holding it firmly in both hands as she concentratedly deciphers its contents. From the little we can see of the room and the light, she seems to be facing a window. The imposing map on the wall directly behind her, only a part of which is visible, seems to symbolise a journey, an absence evoked by this woman alone in her room. Could the absent person be the letter writer?

There are those who have also suggested that the woman is pregnant, as if this could explain the picture's cocoon-like atmosphere. But this would be ignoring the fact that such ample waistlines were fashionable in the 17th century.

Above all, there is the ultramarine of which Vermeer was particularly fond and which – rare in his meagre production – gives this picture its quasi-monochrome aesthetic. Blue is everywhere, from the woman's smock to the chairs and the ribbon on the table. Given the sense of absolute calm created by this scene, the woman's blue garment could almost be a Marian attribute. Or could it be the blue of melancholy? Might the chair beyond her have been suddenly pushed back, as if what she is reading in the letter made her suddenly get up? What could she be reading in this enigmatic missive?

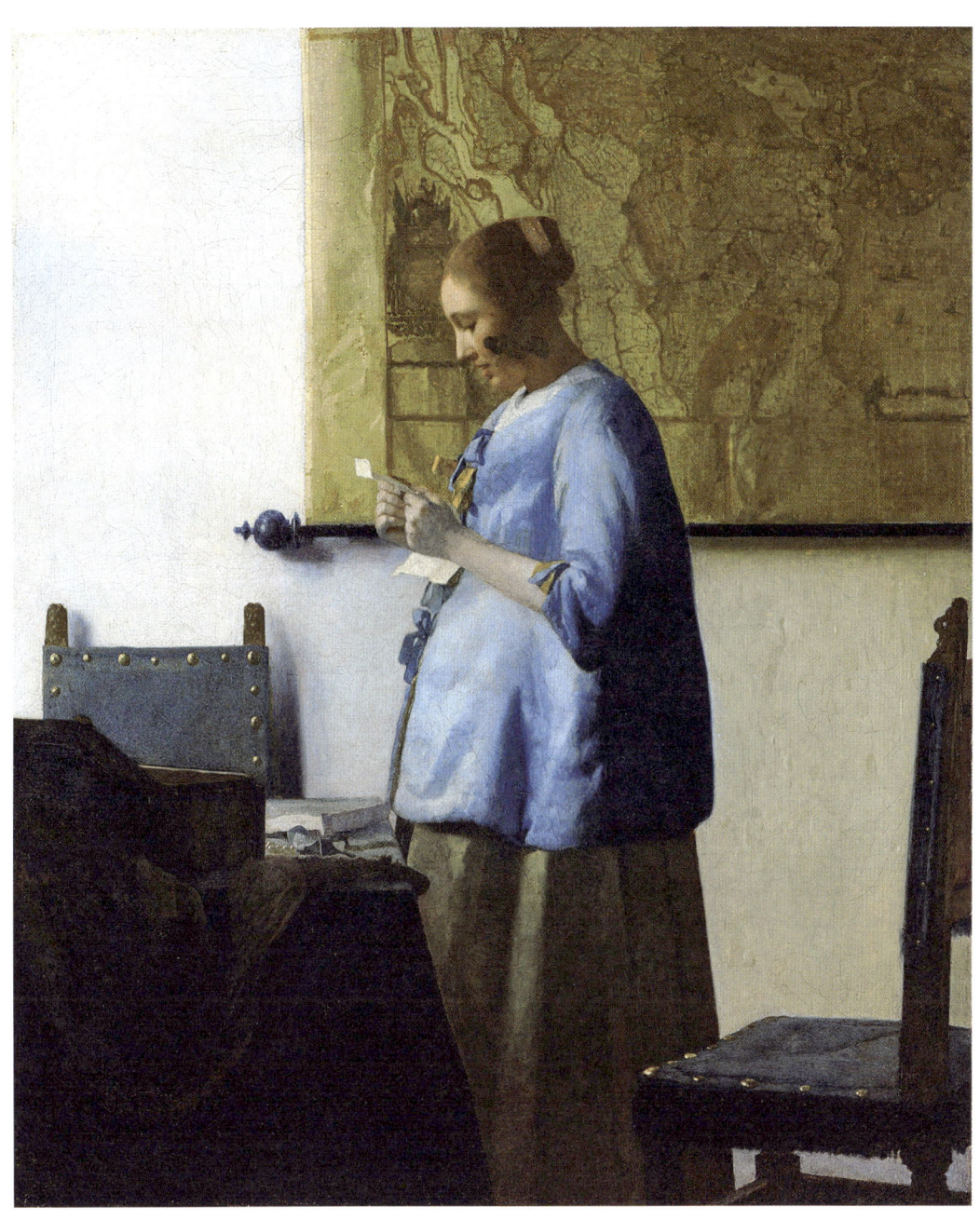

Woman Reading a Letter
Johannes Vermeer (1632–75)
1662/63
Oil on canvas
Rijksmuseum, Amsterdam

Wedding March

Late 18th century

Wedgwood blue

While rococo was still the dominant style in French decorative art, in Great Britain the tendency was for a neoclassical aesthetic inspired by the archaeological discoveries at Herculaneum and Pompeii.

Shortly after founding his ceramics workshop, Josiah Wedgwood opted for simplified forms and a style inherited from antiquity that rapidly boosted his company's fortunes.

In the 1770s he developed jasperware, a kind of semi-porcelain with a very dense, matte paste similar to biscuit that accepted colour throughout the entire body. Light blue jasperware, later called 'Wedgwood blue', rapidly became extraordinarily popular. The characteristic features of this Wedgwood jasperware are its bas-relief decoration, largely inspired by antique art, and its brilliant white decoration contrasting with the blue ground. This ceramic, before its adaptation to production on a larger scale such as vases, was used for small pieces such as medallions and decorative plaques known simply as 'Wedgwood'.

From 1775 on a great many pieces produced by the Wedgwood workshops were created by the sculptor John Flaxman Jr. and inspired by British collections of antique vases.

These very fashionable decorative plaques often had light-hearted, sentimental subjects peopled with plump cherubs, depicted in a naïve style emphasised by the complementary white and Wedgwood blue. This wedding march scene may well have been offered as a symbolic and very fashionable gift to newlyweds.

Wedding March
Decorative plaque
Late 18th century
Wedgwood stoneware
Musée national Adrien-Dubouché,
Limoges

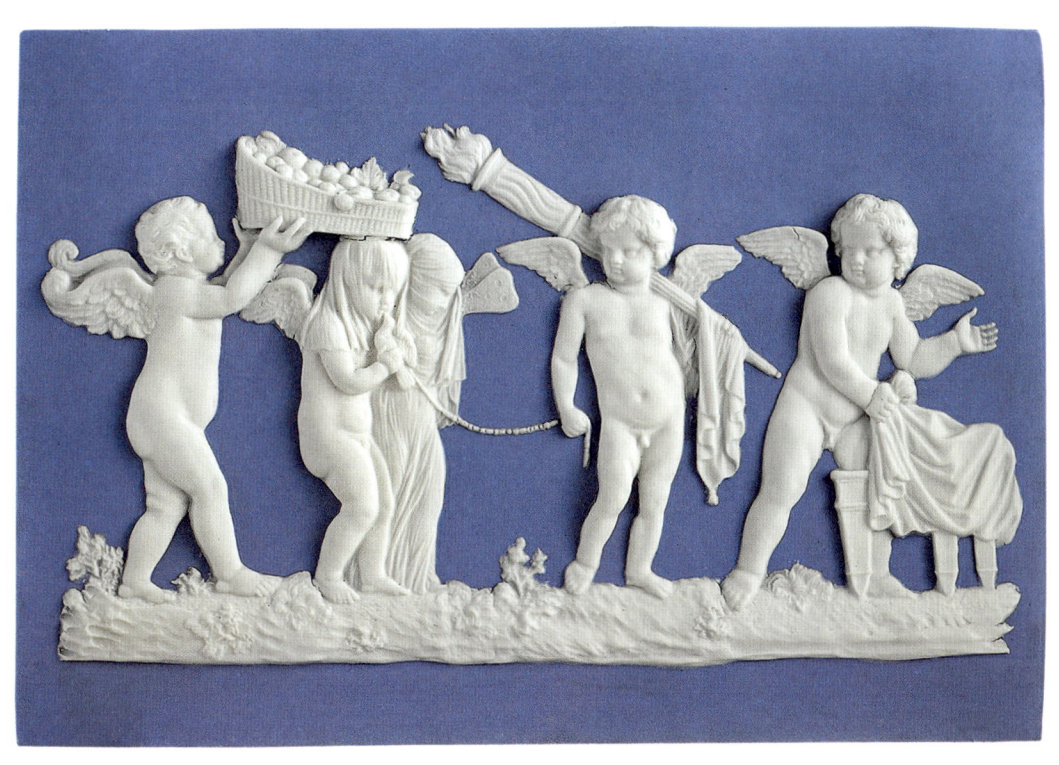

'I find it harder and harder every day
to live up to my blue china'.

Oscar Wilde

The Great Wave off Kanagawa

ca. 1830

Pop Icon

Even Pop culture has been inspired by Hokusai's famous print. The Quiksilver brand used it as its logo and it became a universally accepted pictogram as the emoji signifying 'wave'.

TIMELINE

The Great Wave off Kanagawa as a Source of Inspiration

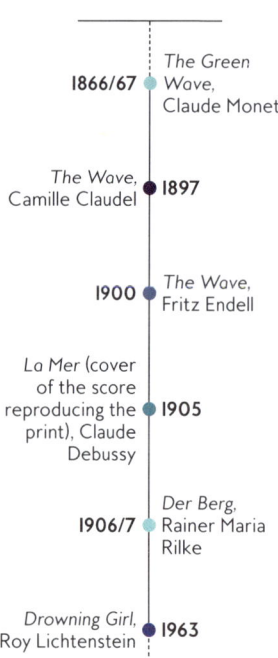

1866/67 — *The Green Wave,* Claude Monet

The Wave, Camille Claudel — **1897**

1900 — *The Wave,* Fritz Endell

La Mer (cover of the score reproducing the print), Claude Debussy — **1905**

1906/7 — *Der Berg,* Rainer Maria Rilke

Drowning Girl, Roy Lichtenstein — **1963**

A Blue Wave

When a prosperous urban bourgeoisie emerged in Japan during the Edo period, to cater for this new public artists depicted subjects that could be mass-produced as prints. This genre became known as *ukiyo-e*, 'images of the floating world'.

Hokusai's *Great Wave* perfectly illustrates the aesthetic of *ukiyo-e* and its reflection on the impermanence of life and nature. This imperious wave, seemingly about to engulf everything in its path, embodies the instability of the world. To make it even more menacing, Hokusai gave its foaming crest clawlike fingers that seem to be reaching down over the boats. The raging sea contrasts with the serene impassivity of Mount Fuji in the distance, in danger of also being submerged yet stoically reassuring us that calm will return after the storm. This impression of tranquillity is strangely accentuated by the boats in the troughs of the waves.

Although this print has become a universal symbol of Japanese art, it contains major western influences. Japanese artists could consult books on Dutch art that were beginning to be imported to Edo, in which they discovered the perspective that Hokusai used here. The blue he chose, Prussian blue, first imported from Germany in 1829, was another recent discovery. Hokusai was one of the first to use it, particularly abundantly in *Thirty-Six Views of Mount Fuji*, the series of prints that includes *The Great Wave*. More intense than the natural indigo previously used in Japanese woodblock prints, Prussian blue enabled much starker contrasts. *The Great Wave* is a perfect synthesis of Western and Eastern art.

'The waves rise up and seem to form the sky,
and their spray touches the lowering clouds'.

Ovid, *Metamorphoses*, Book XI

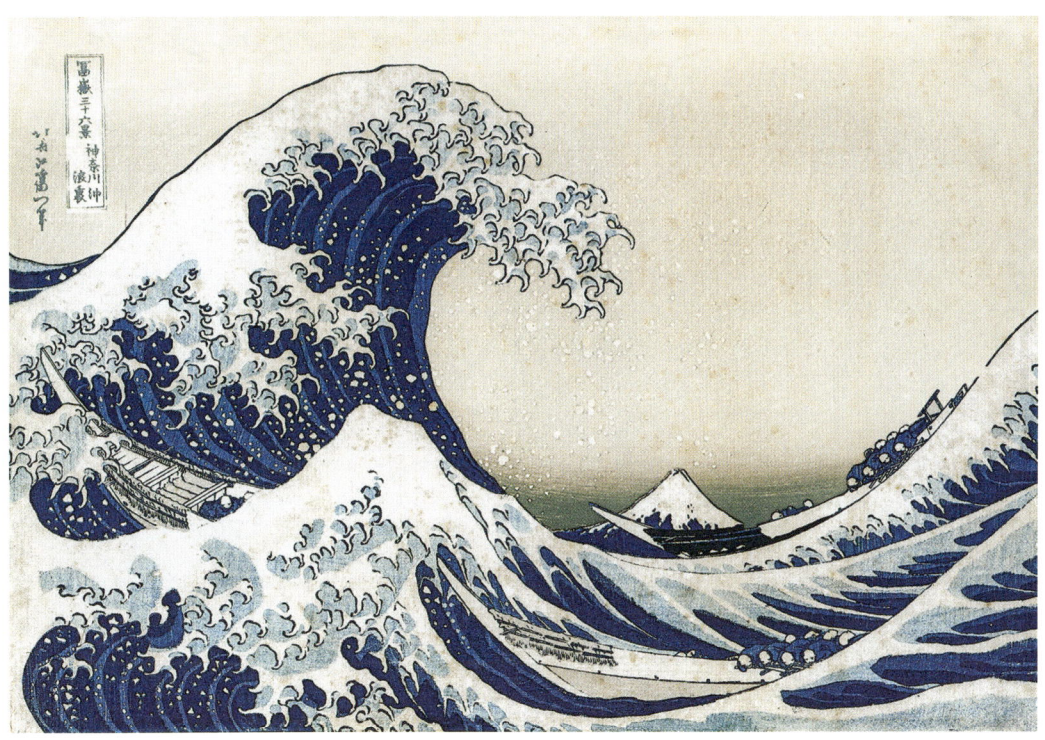

The Great Wave off Kanagawa
Katsushika Hokusai (1760–1849)
ca. 1830
Woodblock print
Private collection

The Starry Night

1889

Van Gogh

In his correspondence in 1885 Van Gogh praised blue and its power: 'Cobalt is a divine colour and there is nothing as fine for putting an atmosphere round things'.

TIMELINE
Step by Step

September 1888 — Café Terrace At Night, Place du Forum, Arles (Otterlo, Kröller-Müller Musem)

Starry Night Over the Rhône (Paris, Musée d'Orsay) — **September 1888**

June 1889 — The Starry Night (Museum of Modern Art, New York)

A Magical Night

In the spring of 1889 Vincent Van Gogh decided to admit himself to an asylum near Saint-Rémy-de-Provence. Having suffered from psychiatric disorders for several years, he infused his work with his feverish torments.

The idea of painting the starry night sky seems to have haunted him and he often wrote about it in his letters. To Émile Bernard he declared: 'But when will I do the Starry Sky, this picture which preoccupies me constantly?' He accomplished this, firstly with *Starry Night Over the Rhône*, then with the more intense *The Starry Night*.

With its long, urgent brushstrokes and sinuous, swirling lines, the picture expresses the agitation haunting the artist's mind. We sense in this image an intense passion verging on chaos but gracefully avoiding it.

To counterbalance the cypress tree like a leaping flame in the foreground and the vertiginous movement of his painterly gestures, Van Gogh fills his night sky with poetry. His stars and his moon fill it with their brilliance, and their haloes pervade the blue night and the landscape. His cosmos has a reassuring glow, like a ray of hope in the darkness of his tormented mind.

Here blue takes on its full mystical, even magical dimension. One has to imagine Van Gogh gazing up into this deep, resplendent, mysterious Provençal night sky. Is he nervous, even suicidal? Does he find some appeasement in it, does he feel infinitely small in front of the immensity of the universe, does he have stars in his eyes?

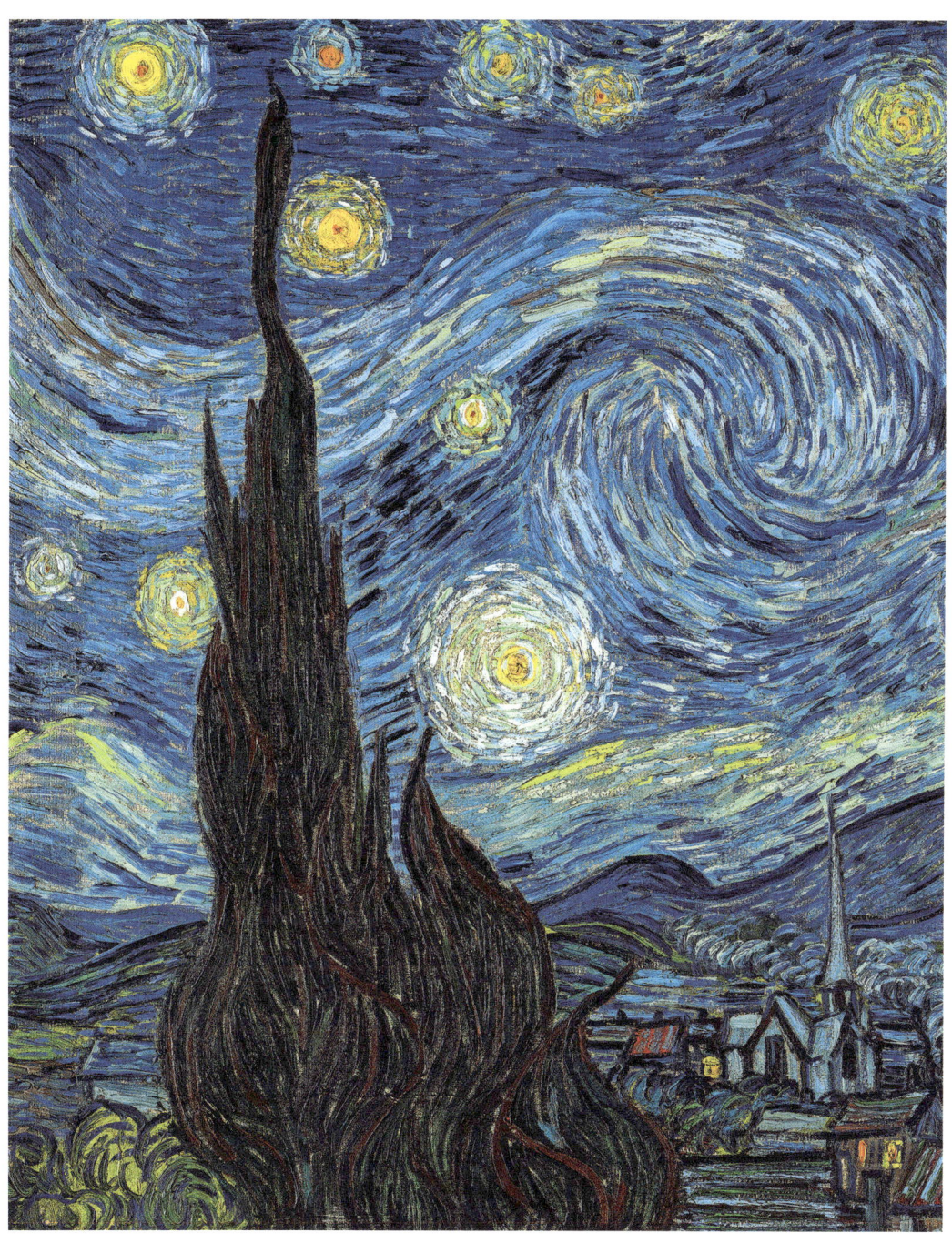

The Starry Night
Vincent Van Gogh (1853–90)
1889
Oil on canvas
Museum of Modern Art, New York

Les Îles d'Or

1891/92

The Big Blue

Pixels

In the 1880s Georges Seurat developed a painting technique employing minute touches of complementary colours. When viewed from a distance, these dots blend visually into shades of other colours. Seurat called this Divisionism, but the critic Félix Fénéon dubbed it 'Pointillism'.

Simultaneous Contrast

This specificity of our perception of colour was first indicated in 1839 by Michel-Eugène Chevreul, who explained that two colours on the same neutral ground appear different if they are juxtaposed. For example, next to a green a yellow will appear slightly red, whereas the same yellow placed next to a red will tend to appear greener.

Henri-Edmond Cross, a recent convert to the Neo-Impressionist Pointillist technique, spent most of his time at Le Lavandou on France's Mediterranean coast, whose seascapes provided him with luminous sources of inspiration.

Using the Pointillist technique, Cross succeeded in giving his works depth by varying the size of their touches of colour, larger in the foreground and smaller and smaller towards the horizon. His technique contravened the principles of Georges Seurat's theory, which considered that the dot should not be visible and never fluctuate in size.

Irrespective of perspective, this variation in size creates a modulation in the work, evoking a current or a sea breeze. The picture's title draws our attention to the islands off the coast at Hyères, visible on the horizon. But what is most important for the artist here is his depiction of the luminous effects and elements blending in this serene, poetic, atmospheric whole.

Sprinkling the blue with lighter touches, Cross creates an even more brilliant light effect, giving the impression that the water is sparkling in the sun. No need for concrete elements to understand this picture, the Mediterranean light and this blue do it all. There we are on a beautiful day, squinting at the dazzling brightness of the sea. Nothing else matters.

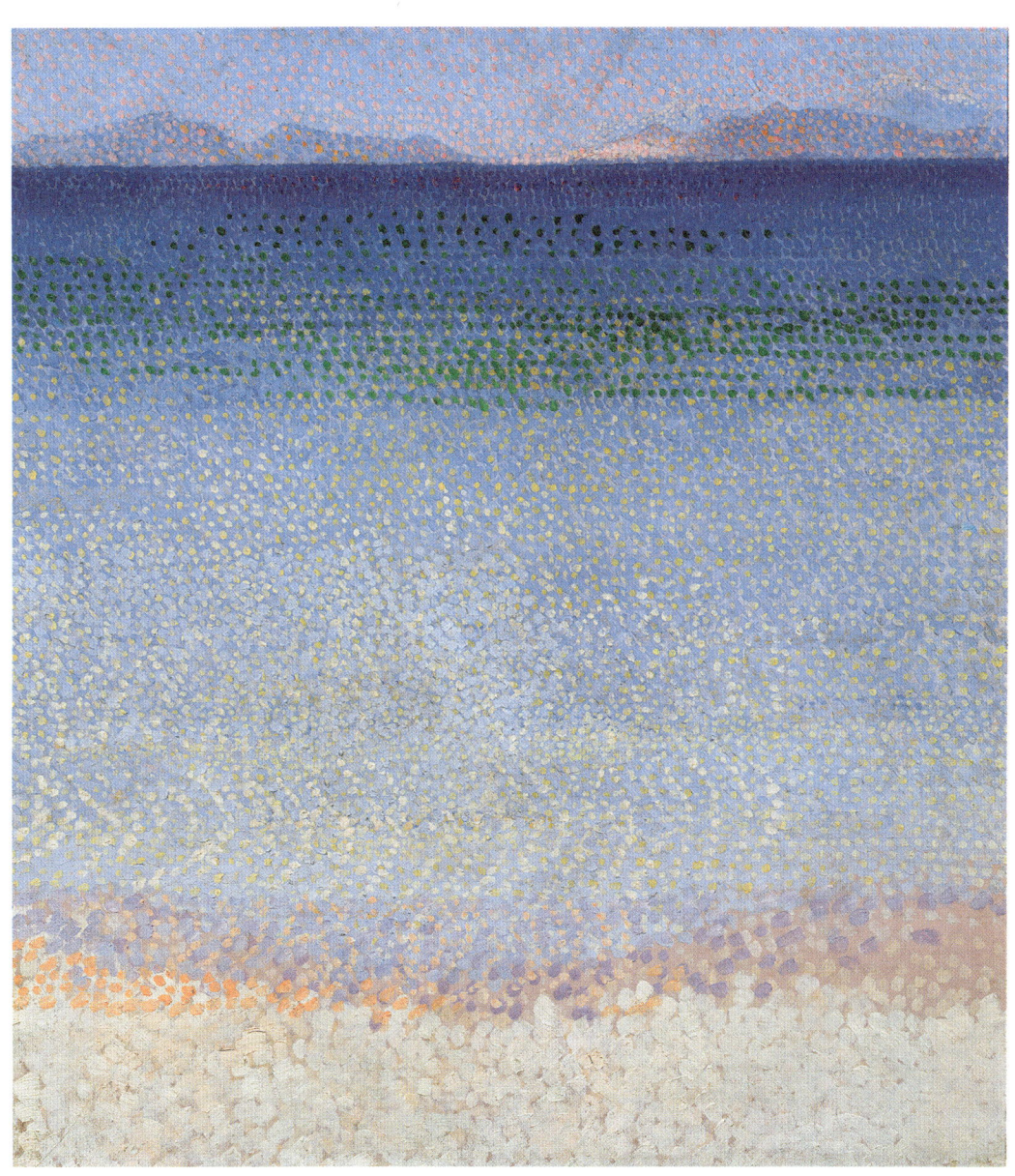

Les Îls d'Or
Henri-Edmond Cross (1856–1910)
1891/92
Oil on canvas
Musée d'Orsay, Paris

Bathers

1894–1905

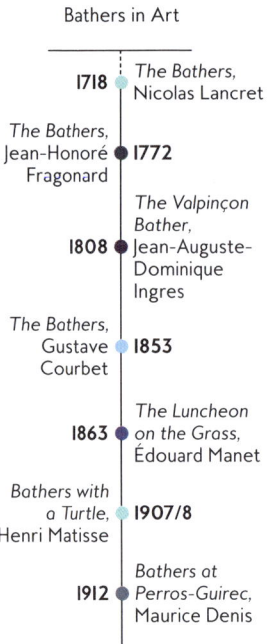

TIMELINE
Bathers in Art

1718	*The Bathers,* Nicolas Lancret
The Bathers, Jean-Honoré Fragonard — 1772	
1808	*The Valpinçon Bather,* Jean-Auguste-Dominique Ingres
The Bathers, Gustave Courbet — 1853	
1863	*The Luncheon on the Grass,* Édouard Manet
Bathers with a Turtle, Henri Matisse — 1907/8	
1912	*Bathers at Perros-Guirec,* Maurice Denis
La Baignade, Pablo Picasso — 1937	

A Return to Nature

Beginning in the 1870s Cézanne painted numerous pictures of female and male bathers. The latest of these works are the large compositions which he constantly reworked until he died and which became his artistic testament for the modernist movements of the early 20th century.

There was nothing new in representing the female nude in a landscape, it has always been a classic theme in painting. But Cézanne's treatent of the subject is very different. First of all, breaking with tradition, he takes no literary or mythological source as subject. His female figures are anonymous bodies whose nudity serves merely as a pretext for his formal concerns.

Cézanne does not differentiate between the scene's components. Landscape and bodies are painted in the same way in distinct areas of colour, all part of a new geometric harmony. The nude body is not an erotic, seductive object but an organic element like the earth and trees. All are one. If there is a trace of sensuality, it is in the flesh of these nudes. They are treated as architectural masses and as such have little to do with anatomical description. Their sensuality lies in their relationship to nature.

Cézanne's palette of blues and greens accentuates this union because their tones incorporate, draw the bodies into the landscape by abolishing the laws of perspective. The artist is showing us a spiritual communion between earth and sky. His simplification of volumes foreshadows Cubism, just as his accentuated contours anticipate Expressionism. By blending man and nature like this Cézanne opened the way for modern art.

'Cézanne was the father of us all'.

Pablo Picasso

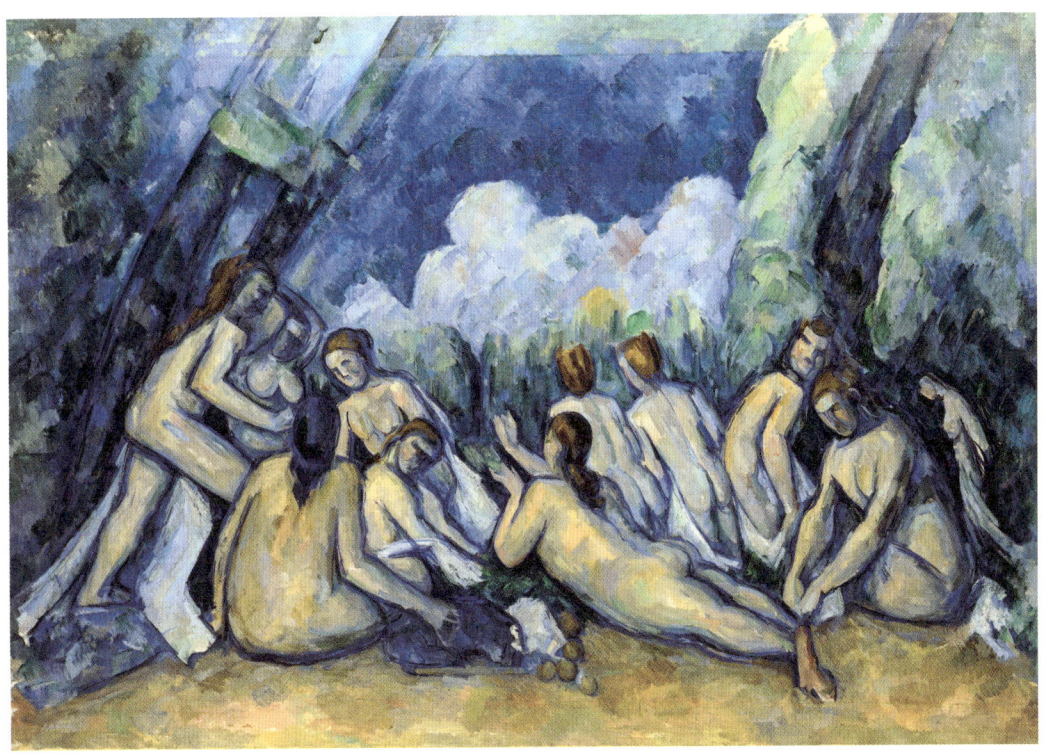

Bathers
Paul Cézanne (1839-1906)
1894-1905
Oil on canvas
National Gallery, London

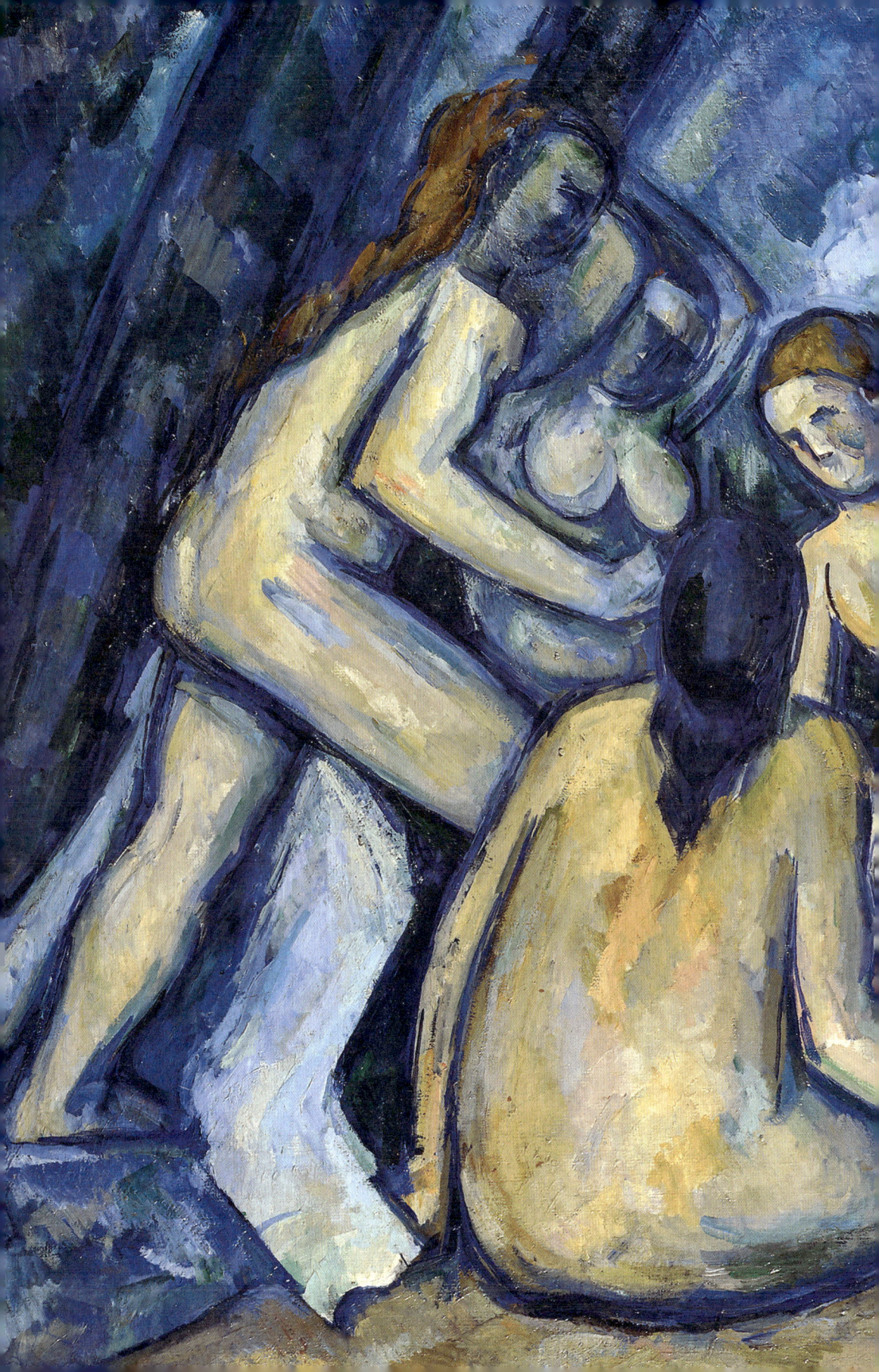

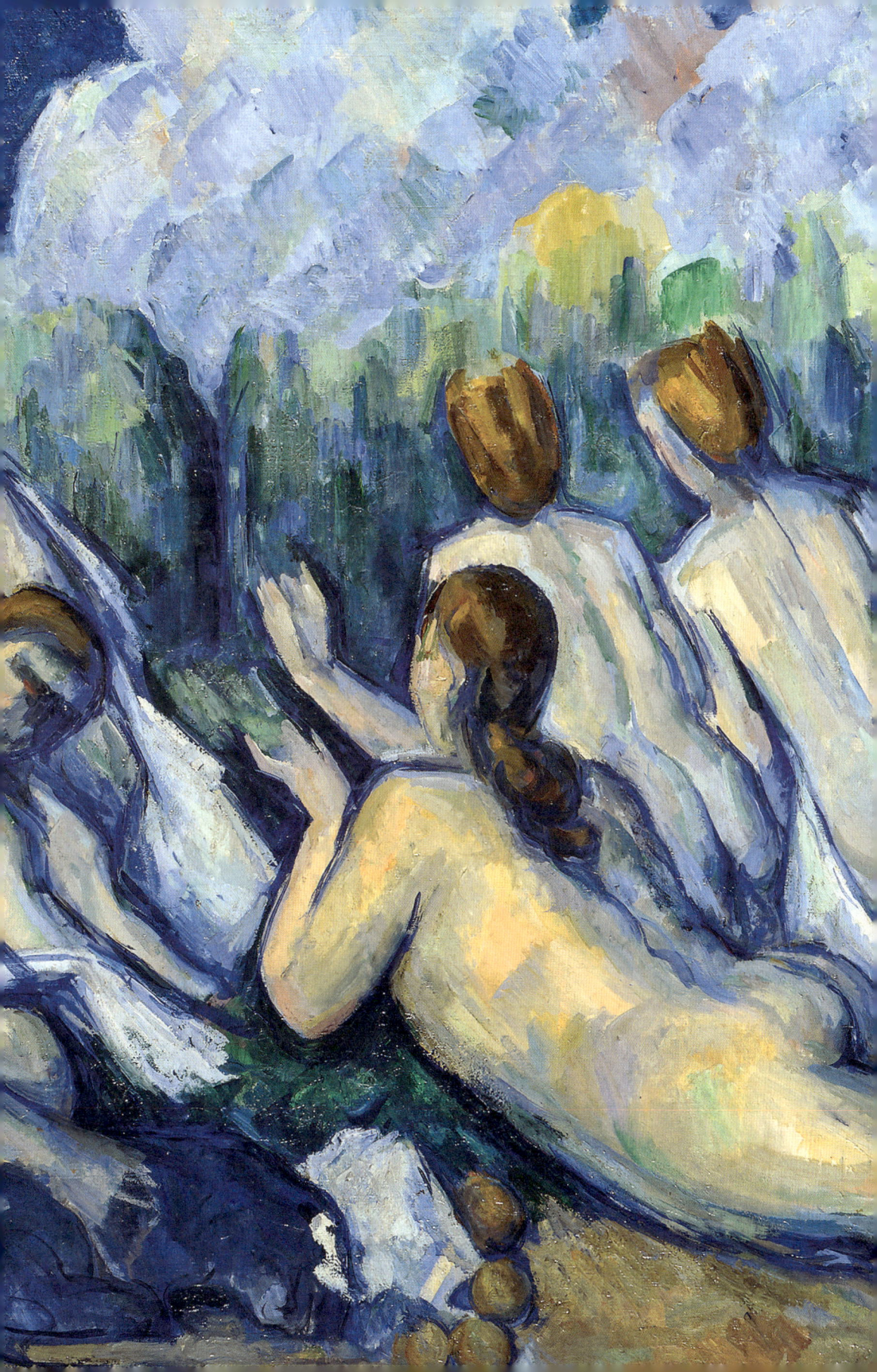

Self-portrait

1901

A Morbid Blue

'It was thinking about Casagemas that got me started painting in blue', Pablo Picasso confided to his friend the journalist, writer and art historian Pierre Daix. And the suicide of his Spanish friend in 1901 did indeed mark the beginning of this melancholic period in his work.

When Picasso painted this self-portrait late in 1901 he portrayed himself as an older man with hollow cheeks and a sallow complexion. Everything suggests that Casagemas's death is haunting him and preventing him from expressing the slightest vitality in his art. Death and suffering are everywhere in his pictures: sick prisoners, bodies in pain, unhappy souls and above all the death of his fellow countryman, depicted in countless drawings and paintings.

In his so-called Blue Period, which endured until 1904, Picasso drew on the styles of other artists, borrowing the areas of flat colour and outlines of Van Gogh and Toulouse-Lautrec, while the poignant evanescence and deformed bodies of a fascinating work like La Vie (1903, Cleveland Museum of Art) evoke El Greco.

Was Picasso devoured by guilt? It is said that Picasso also seduced Germaine, the bewitching model who supposedly drove Casagemas to suicide. So one wonders whether this blue is an expression of mourning or whether it became a fateful cloud that engulfed the artist in his shame. Picasso portrays himself as a ghostlike presence, at one with the almost asphyxiating blue backdrop.

But is it really the blue or rather its treatment that signifies woe here? If one considers his Rose Period, from 1904 to 1906, one cannot say that the artist's gentler colours and happier themes are more joyous. There is still the same melancholy. Can colour really have anything to do with that?

A Friend's View

In an article published in 1905 Guillaume Apollinaire, a close friend of Pablo Picasso's, wrote: 'For a year Picasso lived this painting, wet and blue like the humid depths of the abyss'.

Working by Night

Picasso probably painted this self-portrait at night in his studio by the light of a petrol lamp, a light source that would have changed the surrounding colours and may have played a role in the birth of his Blue Period.

Self-Portrait
Pablo Picasso (1881–1973)
1901
Oil on canvas
Musée national Picasso, Paris

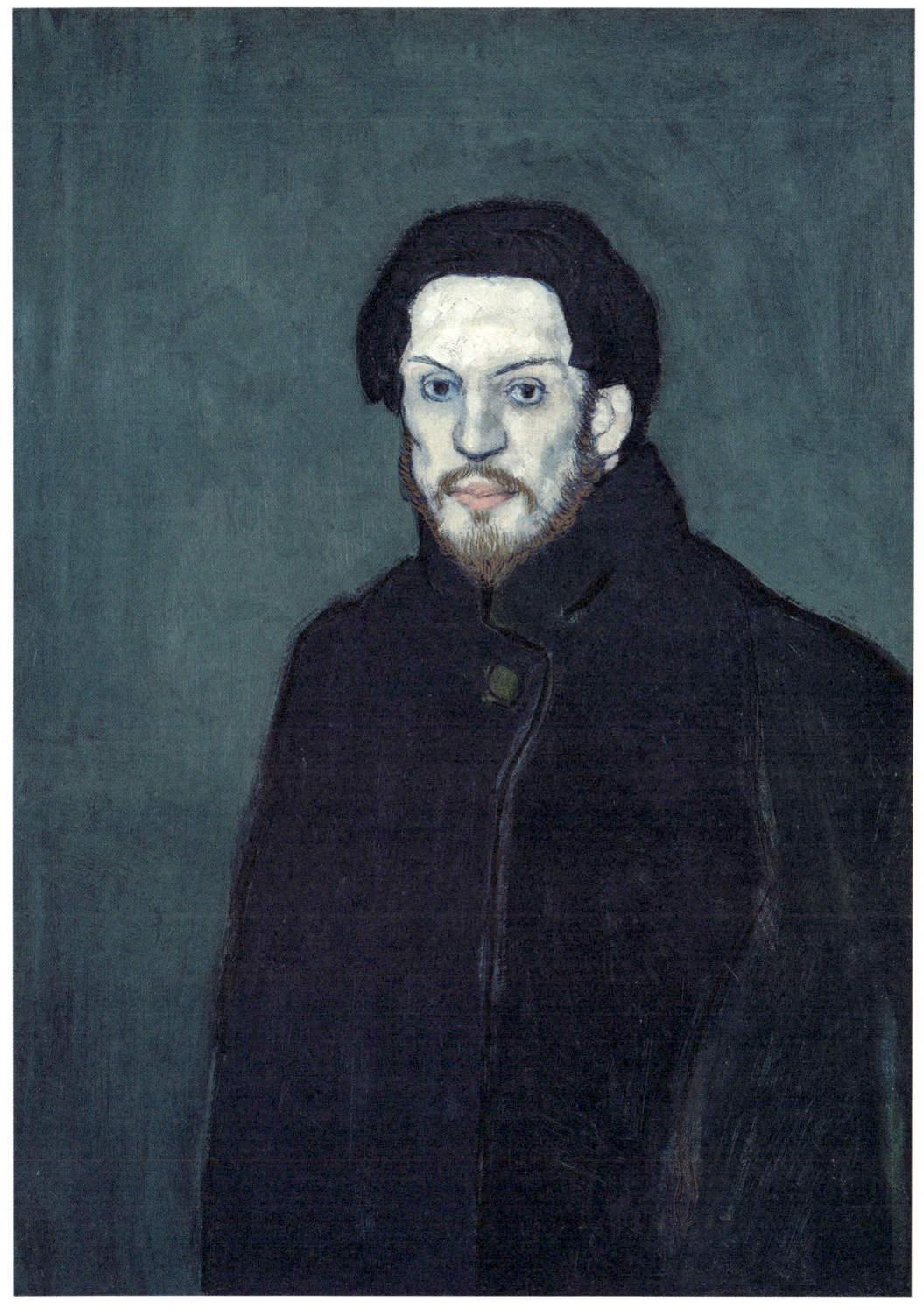

Blue Horse I

1911

Der Blaue Reiter

In 1912, Franz Marc and Wassily Kandinsky published an almanac titled *Der Blaue Reiter*. Their principal aim was to understand the divine essence of the world through art. With their 'blue rider' they were appropriating a mythical romantic figure and associating it with a colour with spiritual connotations. Paul Klee, Robert Delaunay and August Macke were also members of this group. Disrupted by war, Der Blaue Reiter disappeared in 1914.

Branding

The name 'Blue Rider' seems to have been obvious from the outset. Wassily Kandinsky wrote: 'We both liked blue. Marc liked horses and I riders so the name came naturally'.

Blue Horse I
Franz Marc (1880-1916)
1911
Oil on canvas
Städtische Galerie im Lenbachhaus, Munich

A Utopian Refuge

On the front during the First World War, a young German soldier drew. His sketchbooks, discovered after his death in 1916, are full of horses, many of them wounded, symbols of an ideal destroyed by the horrors of the battlefield.

This soldier was Franz Marc, the German painter who with Wassily Kandinsky had founded the expressionist movement Der Blaue Reiter (The Blue Rider) in Munich in 1911. He began by studying philosophy and theology before devoting himself to painting in 1900. His contacts with animal artists prompted him to privilege horses in his work, while from 1905 developing an aesthetic tending toward abstraction.

Franz Marc's passion for horses and his style are reflections of his spirituality: 'Early in my life I found man ugly and animals seemed to me lovelier and purer; but even in them I discovered so much conflict and feeling and such ugliness that instinctively, from inner necessity, my representations became even more schematic and abstract'. His pictures became symbolic universes in which primary colours and animals express emotions and echo human psychology.

Franz Marc developed the theme of the blue horse in several works. Occupying the foreground here is a vigorous, young-looking animal. Its curves echo those of the hills beyond, as if together they form an organic, harmonious and dynamic whole.

In his choice of blue Franz Marc was opting for a mystical, peaceful vocabulary. This is a utopian blue horse embodying the ideal of an absolute world, not the uncertain world on the verge of chaos in the 1910s.

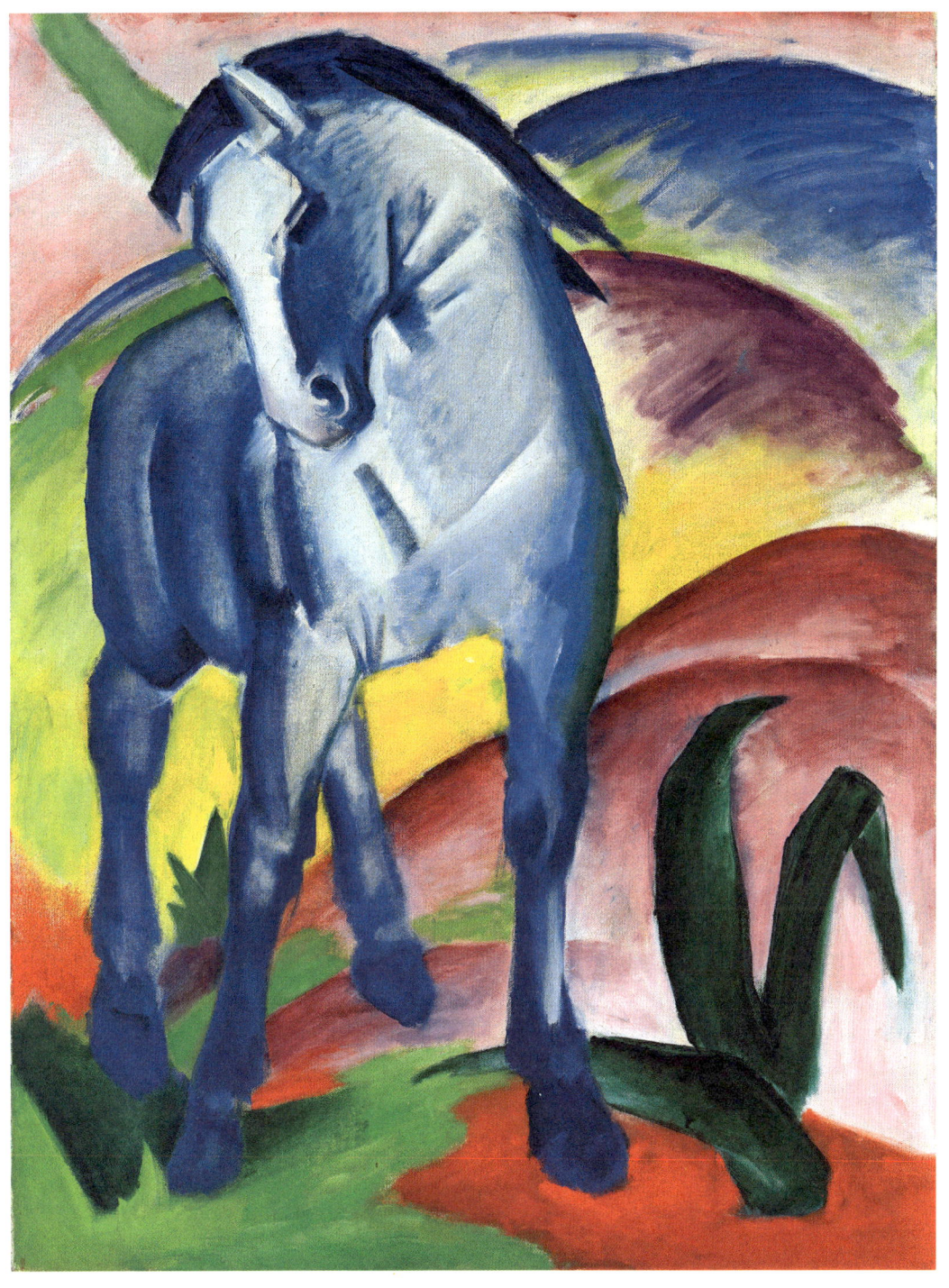

Blue Water Lilies

1916-19

Pacifist Water Lilies

When Claude Monet donated his *Water Lilies* to the French nation after the end of the First World War his artistic garden of Eden became his humanist testament.

A Long-Term Project

Monet's *Water Lilies* series comprises some 250 pictures painted over a period of 31 years. To show them, he tried a variety of exhibition formats and sizes, ranging from square to circular and panoramic.

TIMELINE

Influence of the *Water Lilies*

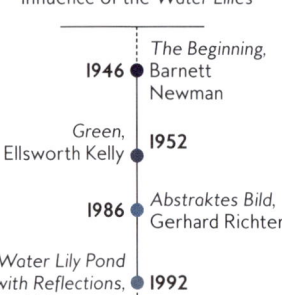

1946 — *The Beginning,* Barnett Newman

Green, Ellsworth Kelly — **1952**

1986 — *Abstraktes Bild,* Gerhard Richter

Water Lily Pond with Reflections, Roy Lichtenstein — **1992**

A Blue Eden

From 1893, on his property at Giverny, Claude Monet created a flower garden and the lily pond that in the 1910s became his prime source of inspiration.

This 'celestial parterre', in Marcel Proust's words, consists of white water lilies (their botanical name is *Nymphaea alba*) surrounded by reeds, weeping willows and wisterias. Claude Monet painted some two hundred and fifty water-lily pictures and this painting is close to the culmination of the formal experimentation he undertook in this series.

A far cry from the shimmering light effects developed by the Impressionists, Monet's painting is now on the verge of abstraction, its mingling planes linking the water, its surface and its iridescence. The vibrating picture surface is created by the reflections of undulating branches and the discreet presence of a few immaculate white lilies. But more than the light it is the blue that seizes our attention and unifies the composition. The picture's square format and focus on a limited space accentuate the sensation of closeness yet play on the impression of infinity. What lies beyond this aquatic universe?

Monet's free brushstrokes and drawing are omni-present, and he even leaves the canvas unpainted around the picture's edges. The *Water Lilies* series is also a means of observing the evolution of the cataracts that eventually deprived Monet of his eyesight. And this is perhaps why these works became increasingly abstract. *Blue Water Lilies* is an example of this: the details are distended and the colour has become quasi-monochrome, poetic, an elemental blue.

'My heart is at Giverny for ever and ever'.

Claude Monet

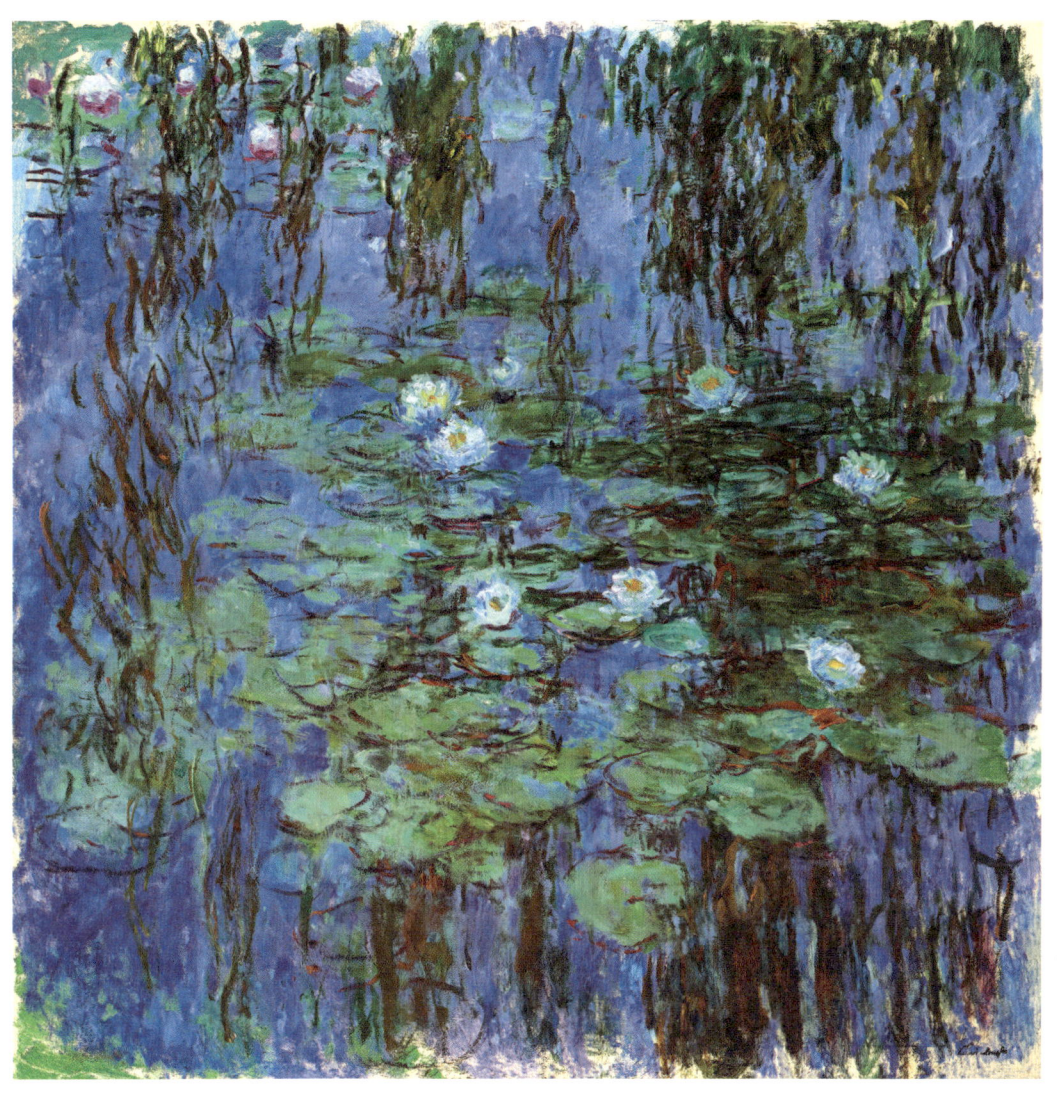

Blue Water Lilies
Claude Monet (1840–1926)
1916–19
Oil on canvas
Musée d'Orsay, Paris

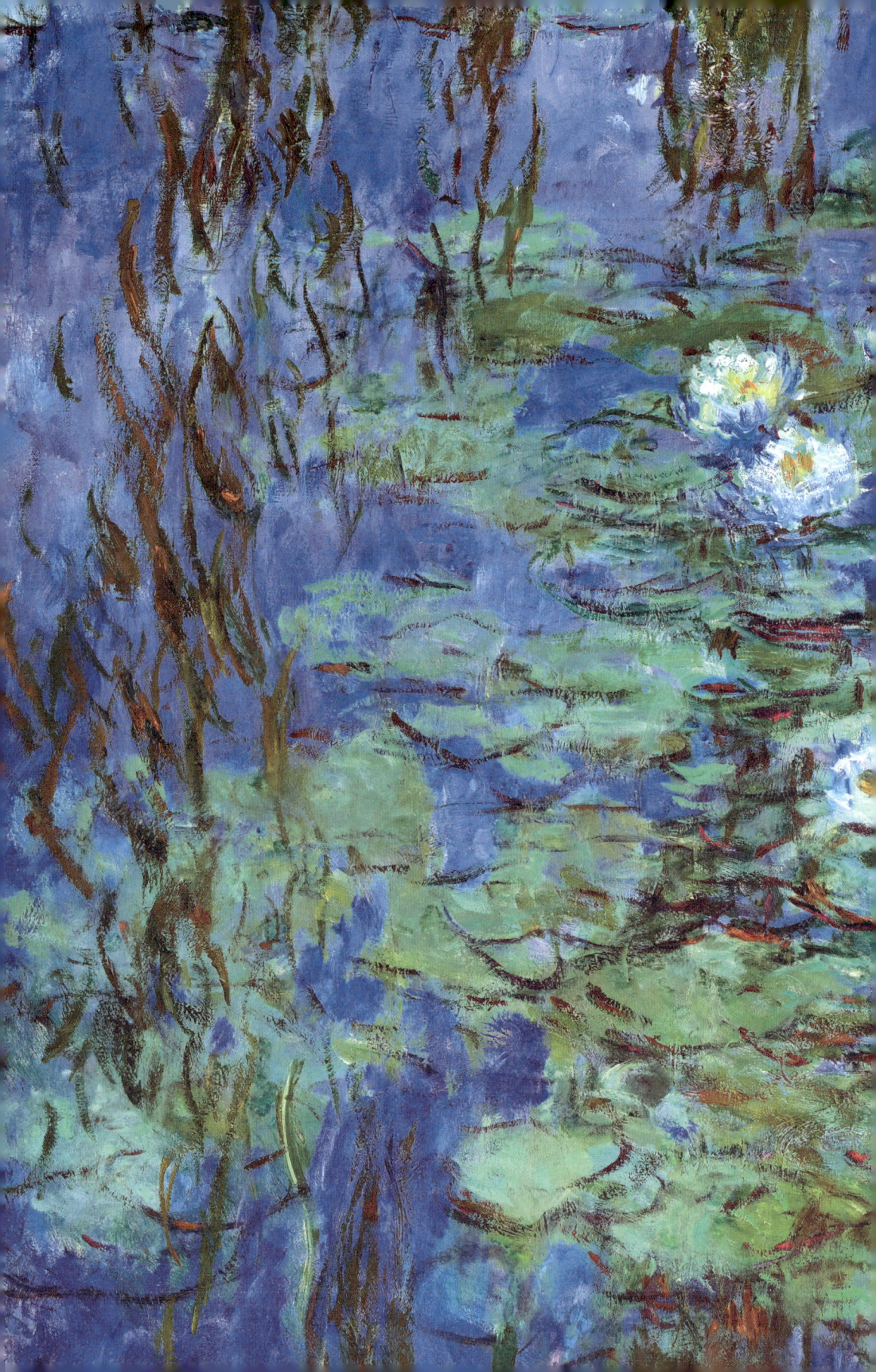

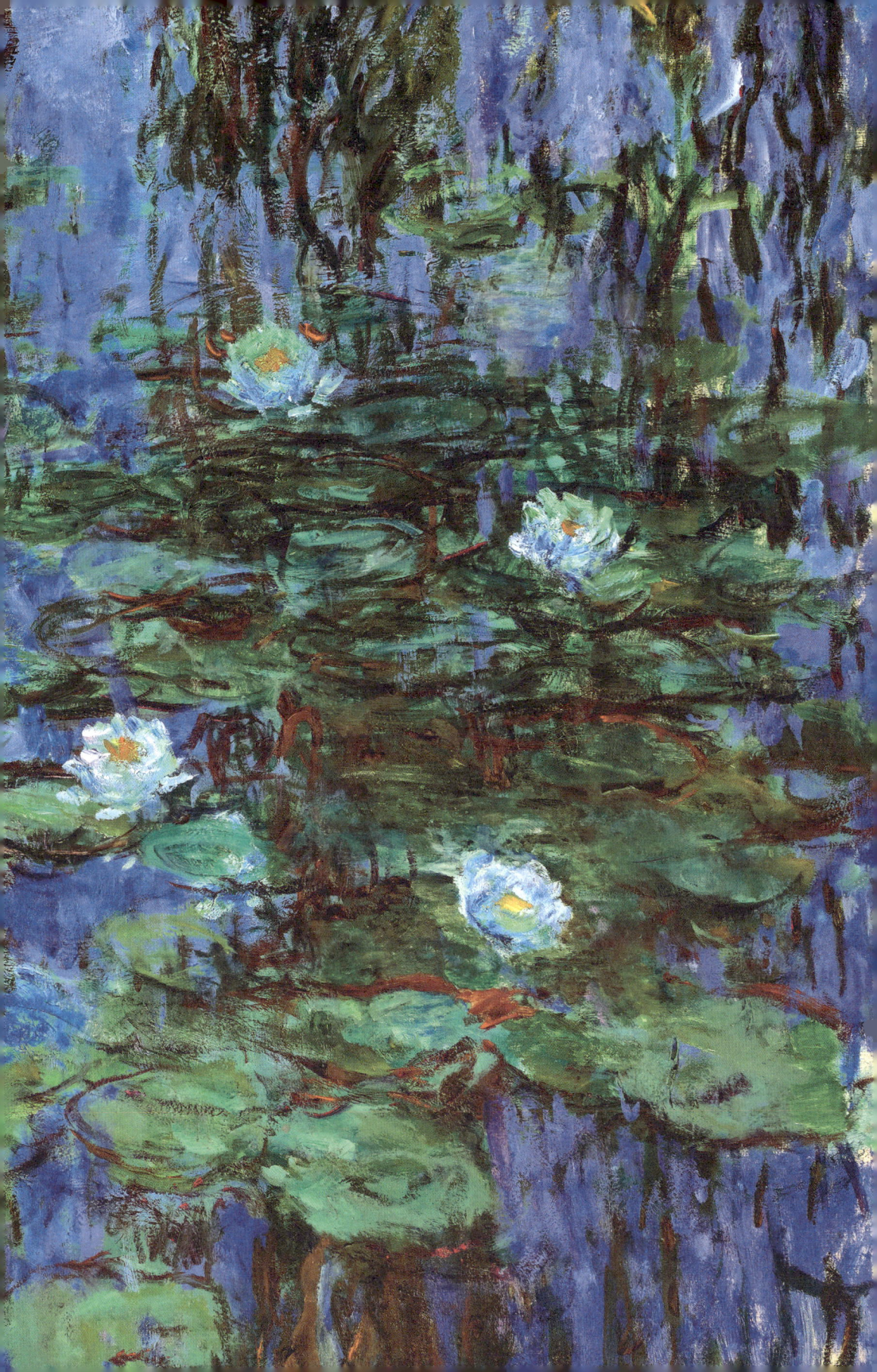

Photo: This is the colour of my dreams

1925

Blue orange

The famous poem by Paul Éluard beginning with the memorable words 'The earth is blue like an orange' was first published in the anthology *L'Amour de la poésie* in 1929.

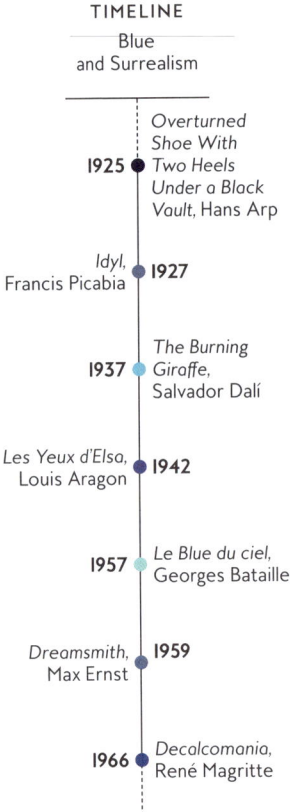

TIMELINE

Blue
and Surrealism

1925 *Overturned Shoe With Two Heels Under a Black Vault*, Hans Arp

Idyl, Francis Picabia **1927**

1937 *The Burning Giraffe,* Salvador Dalí

Les Yeux d'Elsa, Louis Aragon **1942**

1957 *Le Blue du ciel,* Georges Bataille

Dreamsmith, Max Ernst **1959**

1966 *Decalcomania,* René Magritte

Blue Words

Between 1924 and 1928 Joan Miró painted a series of pictures called *Painting-Poems* associating words and symbols. In Paris he adopted the Surrealist ideas of his friends Paul Éluard and André Breton.

Here Miró is proposing a frontal, enigmatic reflexion: on the white paper a word handwritten with the application of a schoolboy and a thick blot of blue paint, beneath which there is the phrase 'This is the colour of my dreams'.

Is Joan Miró really referring to his own dreams? Apart from the anecdote that he never dreamed, or at least never remembered dreans because he slept 'like a mole', his style suggests that it was not so much his dreams that were blue but his inspirations, aspirations and creative process.

With the word 'Photo' Miró is proposing, like the Surrealists, the representation of a photograph; instead of depicting it, why not just name it to make it real? This photo exists in the picture because it tells us it does. And the blue blot becomes the source of Miró's art, the creative departure point, a minute space but one that alone contains all the quasi-mystical palpitation of his work. In this blot masterpieces are born, he senses this. More than a description, 'This is the colour of my dreams' becomes a manifesto.

For blue has a particular meaning for Miró. It is the colour of the sea and sky of his Mediterranean roots, which he transformed in exquisitely poetic abstract works and which culminated in the triptych *Blue* in 1961. And what is the colour of your dreams?

'Yes, the soul has the colour of the gaze.
The blue soul alone carries within it dreams,
it has taken its azure from the waves and
from space'.

Guy de Maupassant

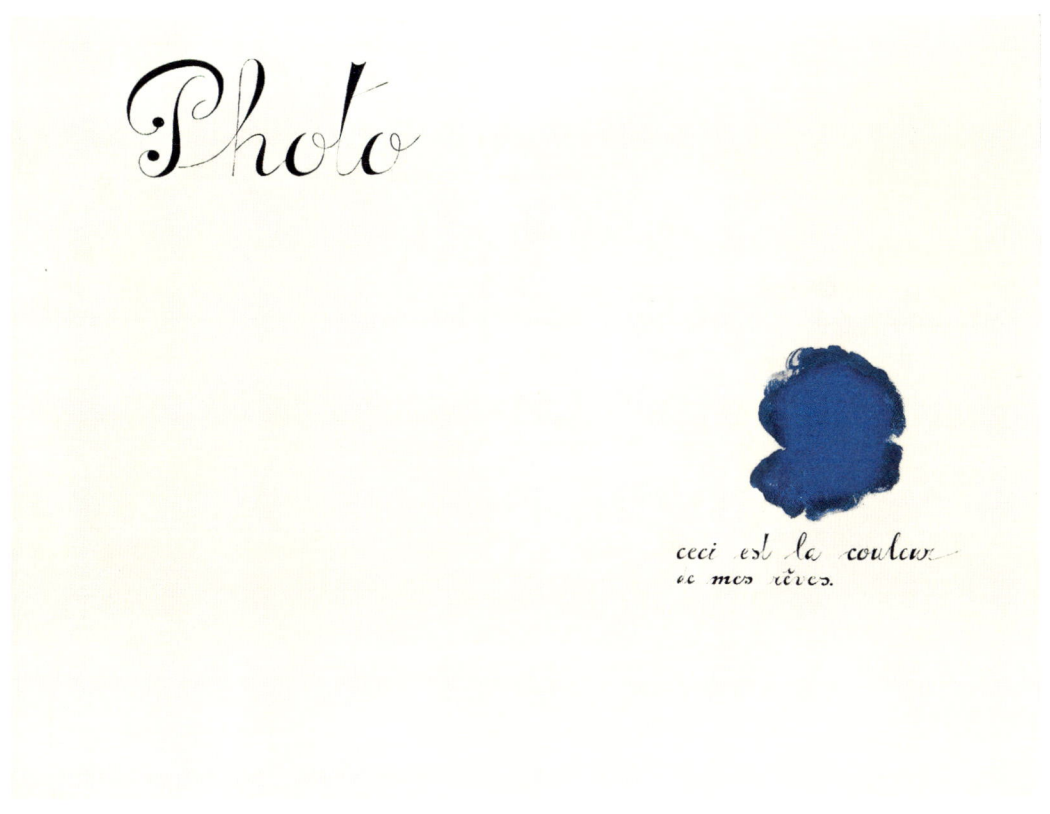

Photo: This is the colour of my dreams
Joan Miró (1893–1983)
1925
Oil and ink on canvas
Pierre Matisse Gallery, New York

Blue Nude III

1952

TIMELINE
Chronology
of the Collages

1929 ● *Dance*

Two Dancers
(curtain for
Massine's ballet
Rouge et Noir) ● 1937-1938

1947 ● *Jazz* (book)

Chapelle
de Vence ● 1949-1951

1952 ● *The Sorrows
of the King*

From Cold to Hot

Beginning in the early 1940s Henri Matisse, bedridden in his room in the Hôtel Régina in Nice, could no longer paint as before. So he began using the gouache cutout technique that he had devised for his preparatory studies for *Dance* in 1929.

In 1943 Matisse began working on the concept of an illustrated book, *Jazz*, composed of gouache. It was published in 1947. This book marked the artist's style until he died.

His series of *Blue Nudes* uses this technique and enabled him to reviit the seated nude pose recurrent in his painted and sculpted works. Matisse, who always admitted his fondness for representing the female nude, succeeded here in reducing it to its most absolute forms, between figuration and abstraction. Using a new artistic tool, a pair of scissors, he could now simplify his drawing to leave only colour.

An interesting aspect of Matisse's *Blue Nude III* is that form and ground seem to have become one. Whereas in his previous paintings he was fond of dense, ornate, colourful backgrounds, his aim here was the conquest of the void. Instead of negating it, he associates it fully with the female figure, allowing it to appear between the body's articulations, like a space of passage, a luminous opening.

Blue is often classified as a cold colour, but by associating it with a sensual nude, Matisse gives it a heat previously denied. And so the female nude becomes the standard bearer of a new definition of blue.

Blue Nude III
Henri Matisse (1869-1954)
1952
Blue gouache on paper cut out and glued to white paper Musée national d'Art moderne, Centre Pompidou, Paris

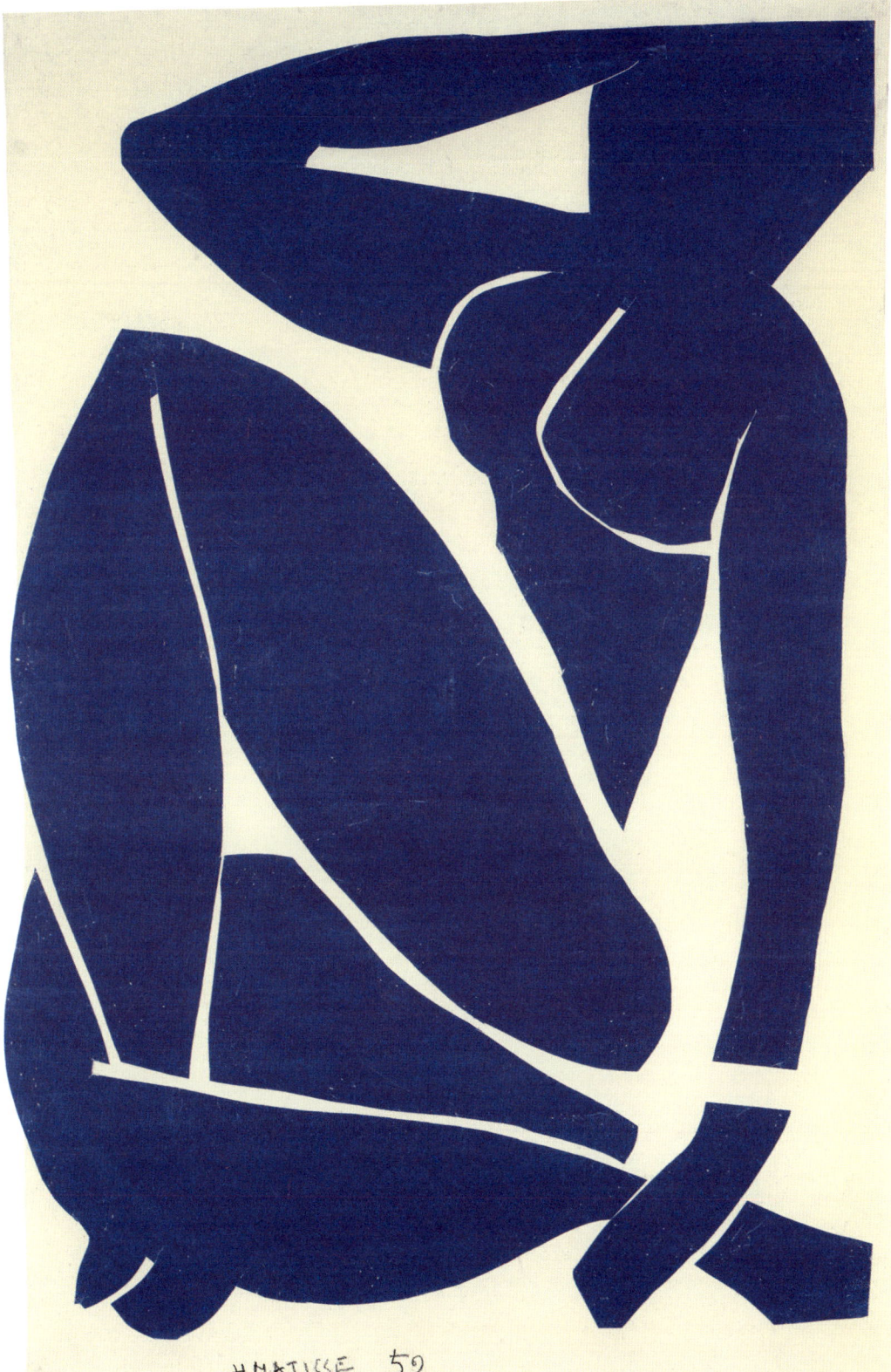

PR I, Portrait-Relief of Arman

1962

His Own Blue

In 1956, in collaboration with the art dealer Edouard Adam and chemists at the Rhône-Poulenc company, Yves Klein devised a pure ultramarine pigment using a synthetic resin. In 1960 he patented the formula of this invention under the name International Klein Blue (IKB). At his marriage in 1962 blue cocktails were served.

Arman

The Franco-American artist Arman met Yves Klein in Nice, at the Judo school they both attended. In the 1950s Arman began a body of work questioning consumer society, notably in his 'accumulations' focussing on the cynical aspect of perishable abundance.

PR I, Portrait-Relief of Arman
Yves Klein (1928–62)
1962
Synthetic resin and pigment on bronze, gold leaf
Musée national d'Art moderne, Centre Pompidou, Paris

Body blue

On a beach in Nice, three young friends 'shared out the world'. Arman took the earth and its riches, Claude Parent the air and Yves Klein the sky and the infinite.

It is hardly surprising that Yves Klein set his sights on the blue sky, on the colour that found its most absolute expression in the monochromes he created starting in 1957. With the blue pigment he patented as IKB now central to his creation, and having taken part in the founding of the Nouveau Réalisme group, he decided in 1960 to produce a series of portrait-reliefs.

He wanted to begin with his friends and fellow Nouveau Réaliste artists: Arman, Claude Parent and Martial Raysse. Intent on using the human body in his art, Yves Klein, who had already employed nude women daubed with blue paint, took plaster moulds of his subjects down to the knees. He then cast them in bronze and spray painted them with his blue pigment. Only his portrait-relief of Arman was finished. Klein had a passion for philosophy and spirituality and his work is full of his esoteric thoughts. Here, like his blue signature colour, the gold ground creates a mystical, priceless aura with a definite dreamlike dimension.

Nevertheless, as if Klein wanted to bring the spiritual into the earthly world, this portrait of his friend is strikingly real. Arman's clenched fists and frowning gaze are an affirmation of vitality contrasting with the funerary impression created by the golden shroud and blue 'statue'. These forces of life, death and the divine now seem almost ironic when one considers that Klein died of a heart attack shortly afterwards.

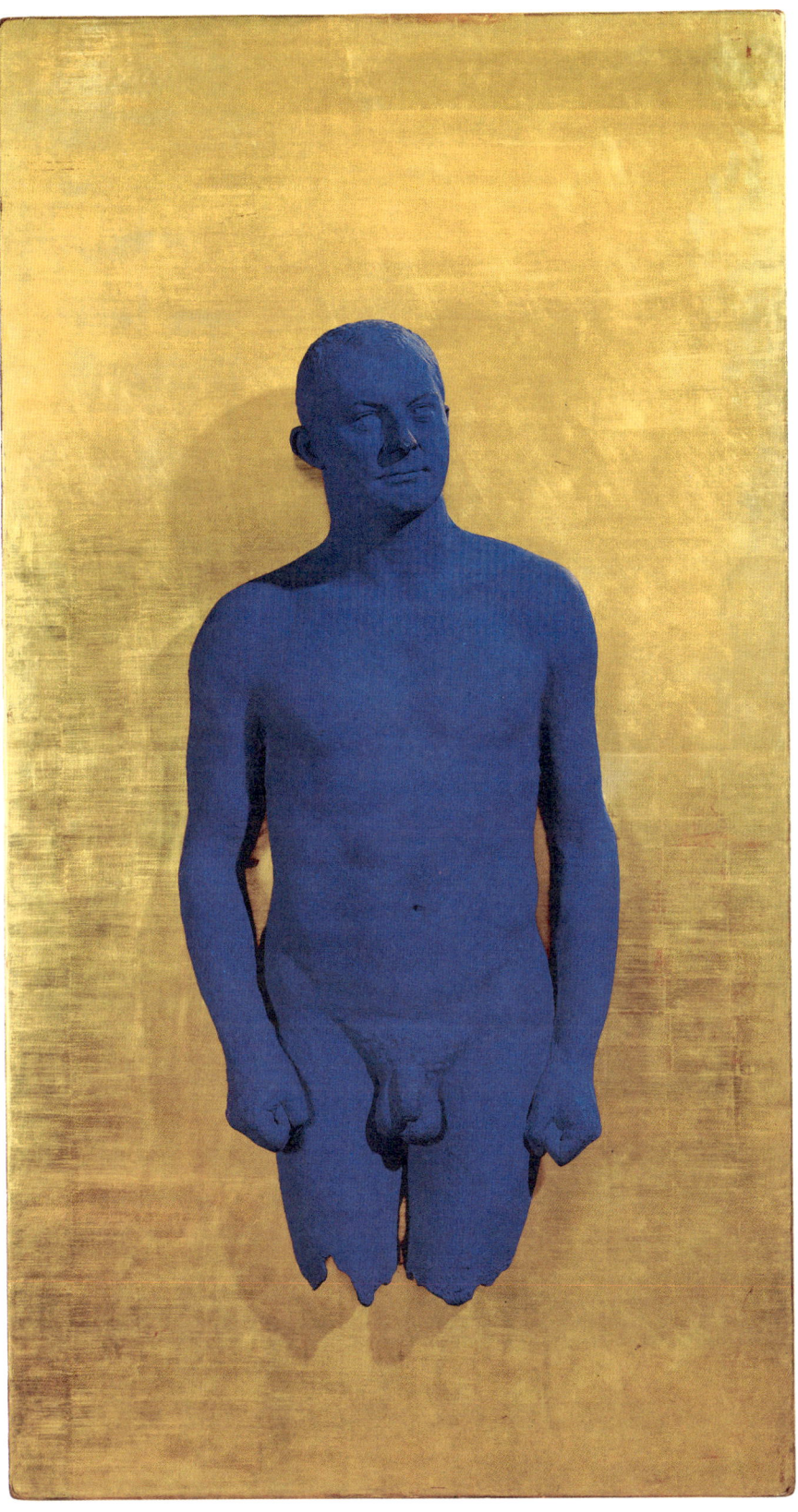

A Bigger Splash

1967

Swimming Pools

David Hockney is as
closely associated with
swimming pools as Claude
Monet is with water lilies.
Even if they only represent
a fraction of his artistic
output, they have become
iconic – he even created
an underwater fresco for
the renovated swimming
pool of the Hollywood
Roosevelt Hotel
(Los Angeles, 1988).

TIMELINE
Swimming Pools in Art

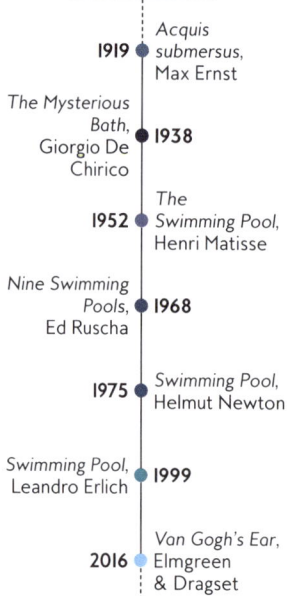

1919	*Acquis submersus,* Max Ernst
The Mysterious Bath, Giorgio De Chirico	1938
1952	*The Swimming Pool,* Henri Matisse
Nine Swimming Pools, Ed Ruscha	1968
1975	*Swimming Pool,* Helmut Newton
Swimming Pool, Leandro Erlich	1999
2016	*Van Gogh's Ear,* Elmgreen & Dragset

To the Bottom of the Pool

**The sun is so hot so you dive into the pool … David
Hockney turns a trivial sun-drenched holiday moment
into an (ironic?) metaphor of the optimism of the
1960s.**

The British artist was in Los Angeles when he painted
this picture. He was fascinated by how many swimming
pools there were everywhere in the city, especially since
having one in his home country was a luxury and above all
incompatible with the climate.

David Hockney based *A Bigger Splash* on a photograph
of a swimming pool in a book, while the building in the
background is inspired by Californian architecture. The
entire picture surface is composed of areas of flat colour
and dominated by horizontals, with the two tall palm
trees as its only vertical elements.

The blue sky and blue pool are separated by the pale-
coloured house and terrace blocking the horizon, which
might otherwise have been infinitely distant. But above all
there is the turquoise water of the pool in the foreground,
into which we are invited to plunge from the contrasting
yellow diving board. But the plume of water rising from
the water suggests we may have already done so.

Everything in this image symbolises optimism – the acidic
colours, the radiant weather, the diving board – and yet
something is wrong. Everything is too perfect, like a
cardboard décor, and the absence of human presence is
unsettling, albeit evoked by the omnipresent splash
frozen in the void. Suddenly this Californian blue hits us
and fills us with anxiety. The swimming pool is both a
place of pleasure and disquiet, as in *La Piscine*, the iconic
film starring Romy Schneider and Alain Delon released
in 1969.

'I love California, everything is so artificial'.

David Hockney

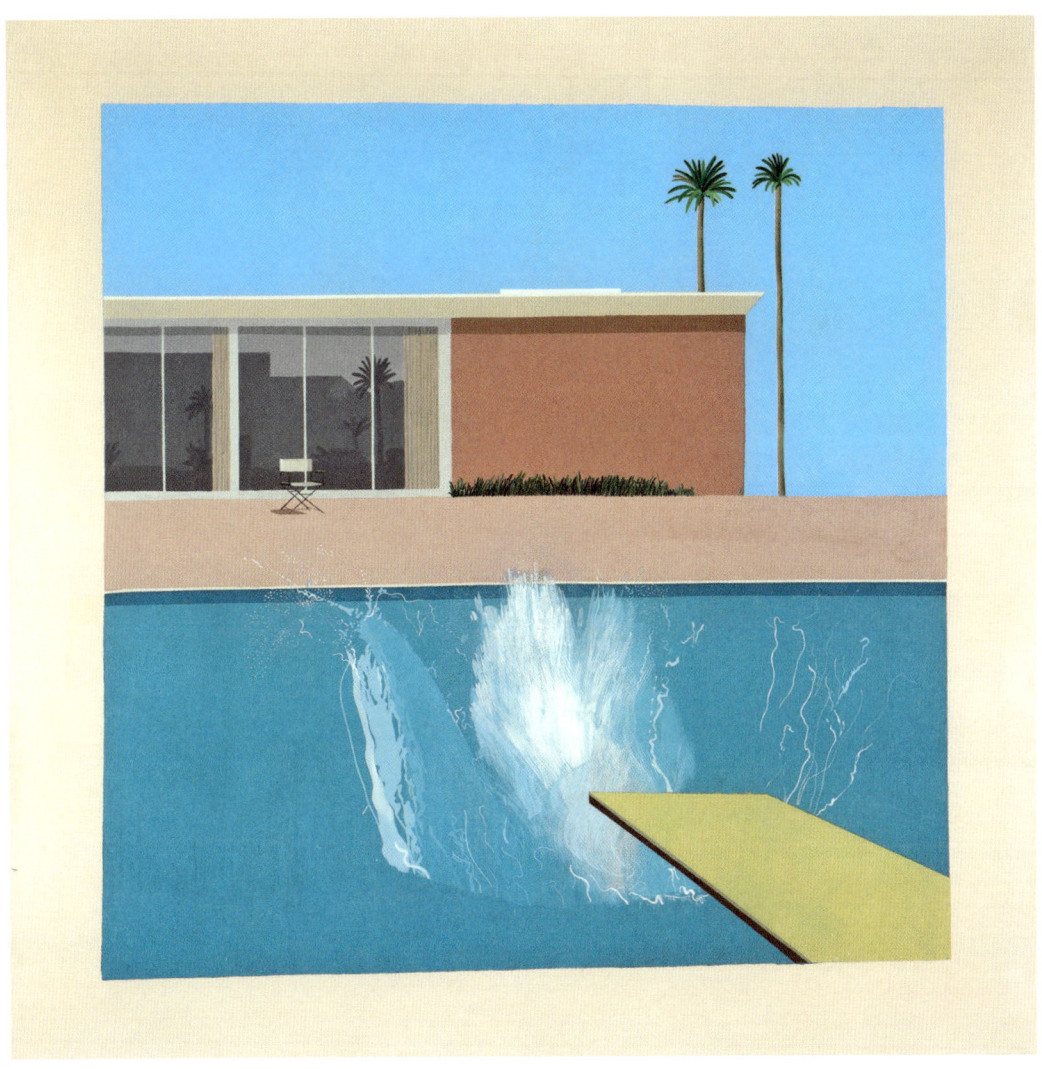

A Bigger Splash
David Hockney (born 1937)
1967
Acrylic on canvas
Tate Collection, London

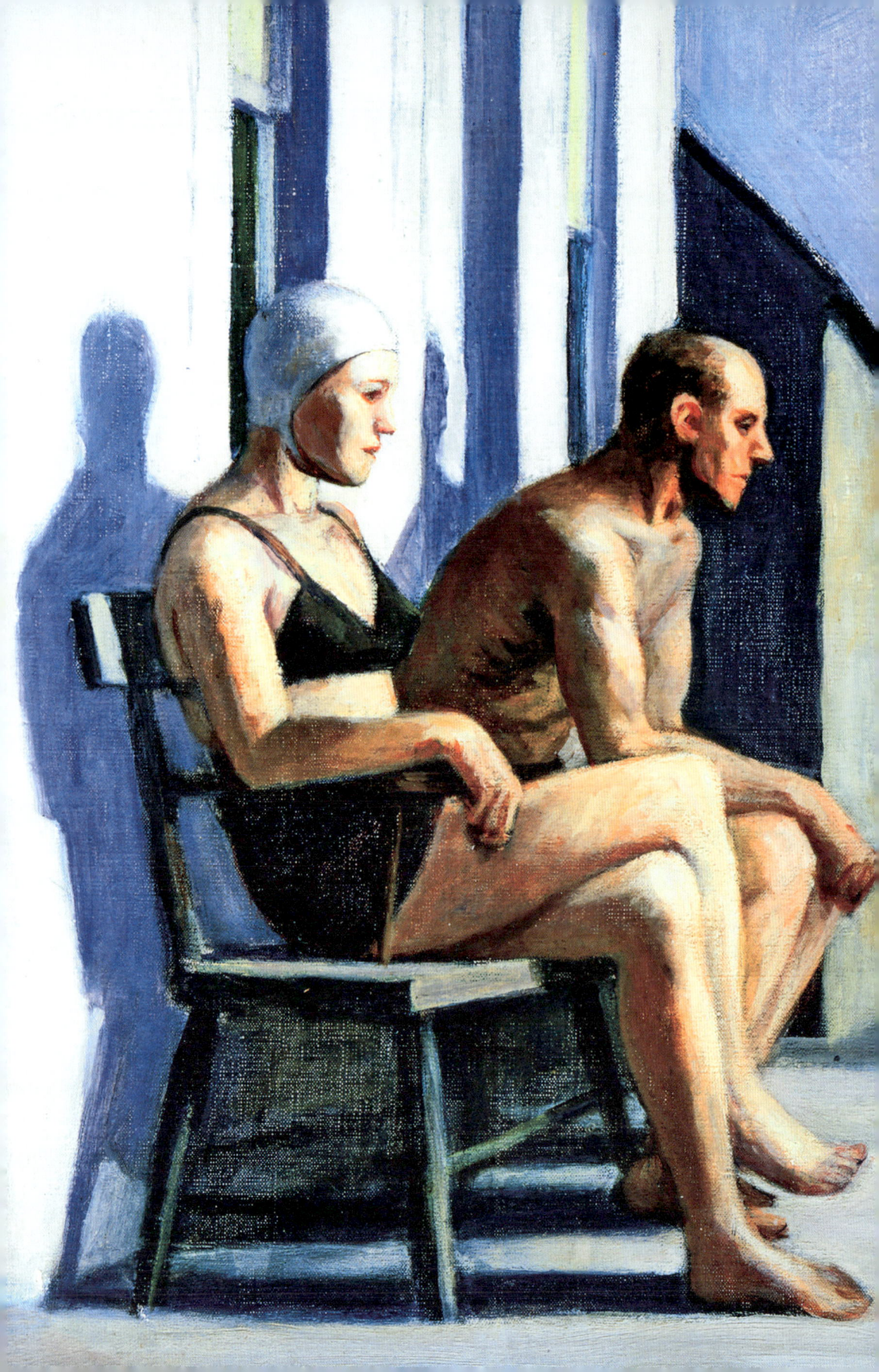

THE
LESS EXPECTED

—

The Ishtar Gate

ca. 580 B.C.

The Gates of the Gods

Babylon

This Mesopotamian city on the Euphrates, some 100 kilometres from Baghdad in present-day Iraq, had its heyday during the reign of Nebuchadnezzar II. The city, one of the largest in the ancient world, was renowned far and wide for its towering walls, hanging gardens and its ziggurat, which may have inspired the myth of the Tower of Babel.

A Few Babylonian Deities
—
Adad, god of storms and rain; Ea (or Enki), god of subterranean waters; Gilgamesh, king, semi-legendary hero with superhuman exploits; Ishtar, goddess of love and war; Nergal, master of the dead and Hell; Marduk, Babylonian creator god; Shamash, sun god and god of justice

One could enter the city of Babylon through one of its eight gates built by order of King Nebuchadnezzar II. Each bore the name of a god or goddess and was the departure point for processions venerating these deities.

To the north of the city, the imposing Ishtar Gate was dedicated to the goddess of the same name, symbol of fertility and love but also victory. Its dazzling decoration is composed of deep-blue glazed bricks and bas-reliefs depicting animals. The purpose of these creatures was to protect Babylon by intimidating and repelling evil spirits venturing into the vicinity. Depicted here are a bull, symbol of Adad, a god with power over storms, and a dragon, allegory of Marduk, supreme god of the pantheon.

The Ishtar Gate is composed of glazed bricks coloured with lapis lazuli, readily available in the region. Artisans then knew of and perhaps used the recipe for Egyptian blue (p. 16), but the choice of lapis lazuli was no coincidence due to its important significations. It was above all a symbol of the heavens and supernatural life and acted as a talisman. The grandiose, intense blue gate represented the passage between two earthly entities, the interior and exterior of the city.

Thanks to excavations by German archaeologists beginning at the very end of the 19th century, part of the Ishtar Gate - 26 metres wide and 15 metres high - was later reconstructed stone by stone in the Pergamonmuseum in Berlin. The other part, in Baghdad, continues, as much as possible, its role as guardian against the vicissitudes of war.

The Ishtar Gate (detail)
ca. 580 B.C.
Glazed bricks
Pergamonmuseum, Berlin

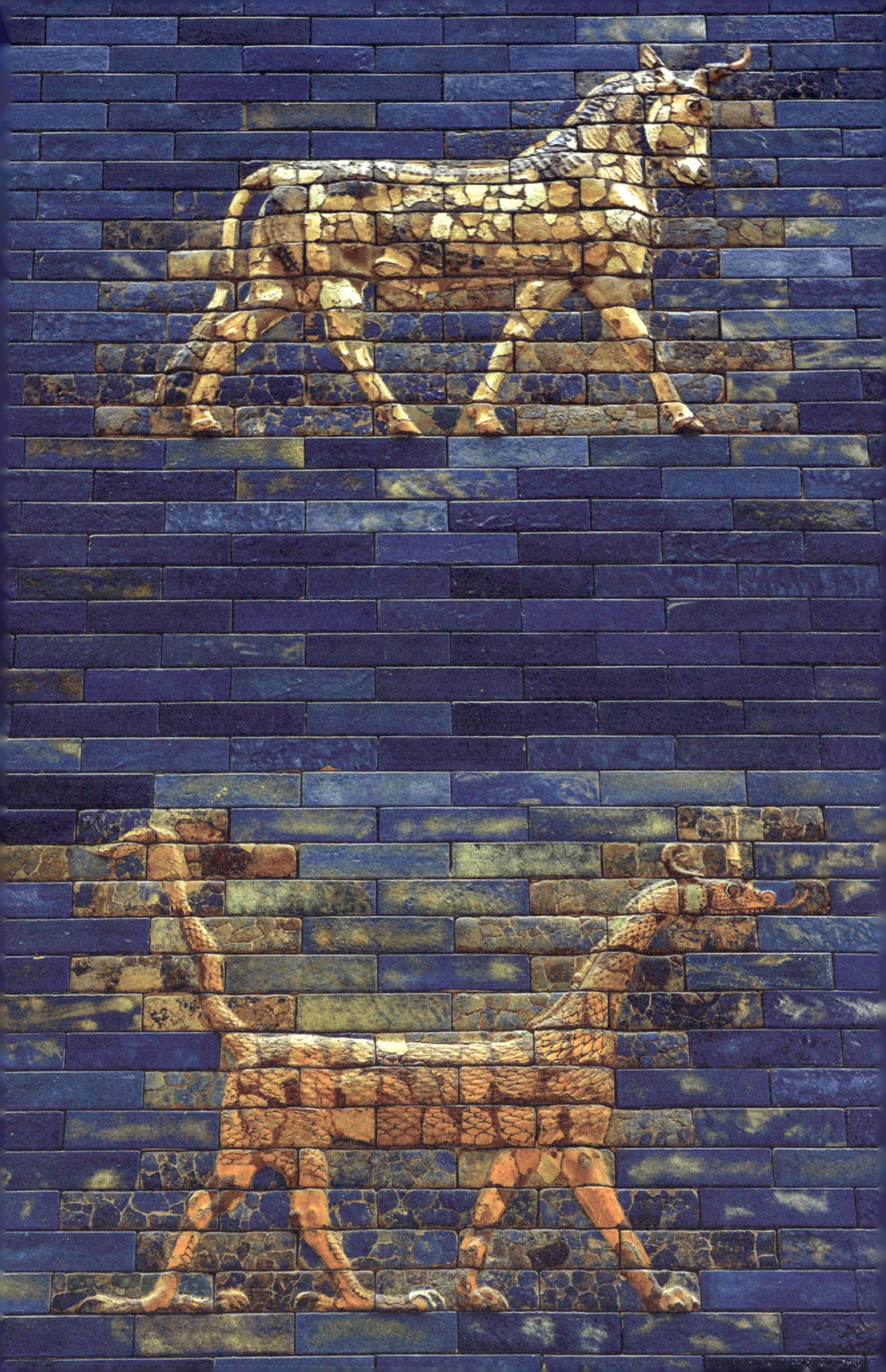

Diana

1st century B.C.

A Name Change

The Romans associated blue with the barbarians, and the ancient Greeks used it very rarely. Hence the conclusion that ancient peoples, except for the Egyptians, had an aversion to blue and that the Greeks were even incapable of seeing it.

The colour blue being absent from literary works in antiquity, 19th-century scholars deduced that our distant ancestors must have suffered from a visual deficiency preventing them from seeing blue hues. Fortunately, archaeology was able to contradict such far-fetched notions. Before Pompeii and Herculaneum diverted international attention, the French undertook excavations in the Roman port of Stabiae at the foot of Vesuvius.

In the middle of Villa Arianna, named after the remains of a fresco showing Diana sleeping, this depiction of the goddess of the hunt was also unearthed. In a similar manner to her representations on Greek vases she is depicted as she is about to draw her bow, yet despite this warriorlike pose, her face is calm and peaceful.

Painted on an azure ground, this fresco affirms that blue was indeed used in Roman antiquity. The background hue is very similar to Egyptian blue, suggesting that that technique may have spread abroad. And because the artworks buried under the lava of Vesuvius have spawned many fantasies, it is hardly surprising that 19th-century art historians preferred to give Egyptian blue the much more evocative name Pompeian blue.

The Antique Theory of Colours

The lack of popularity of blue in ancient Greece and the Roman Empire may have been due to the ancient theory of colours. Colours were classified on a scale of luminosity, with white and black the extremities and the intermediate colours ranging from light to dark. It was the perception and brilliance of a colour that defined its value. Under this system blue was close to black.

Painting
affresco

The word 'fresco' comes from the Italian *affresco*, meaning 'fresh'. It denotes a mural technique of painting on damp lime plaster. As the plaster dries it absorbs the pigments to form a hard and durable painted surface.

Diana
1st century B.C.
Fresco
Museo Archeologico Nationale, Naples

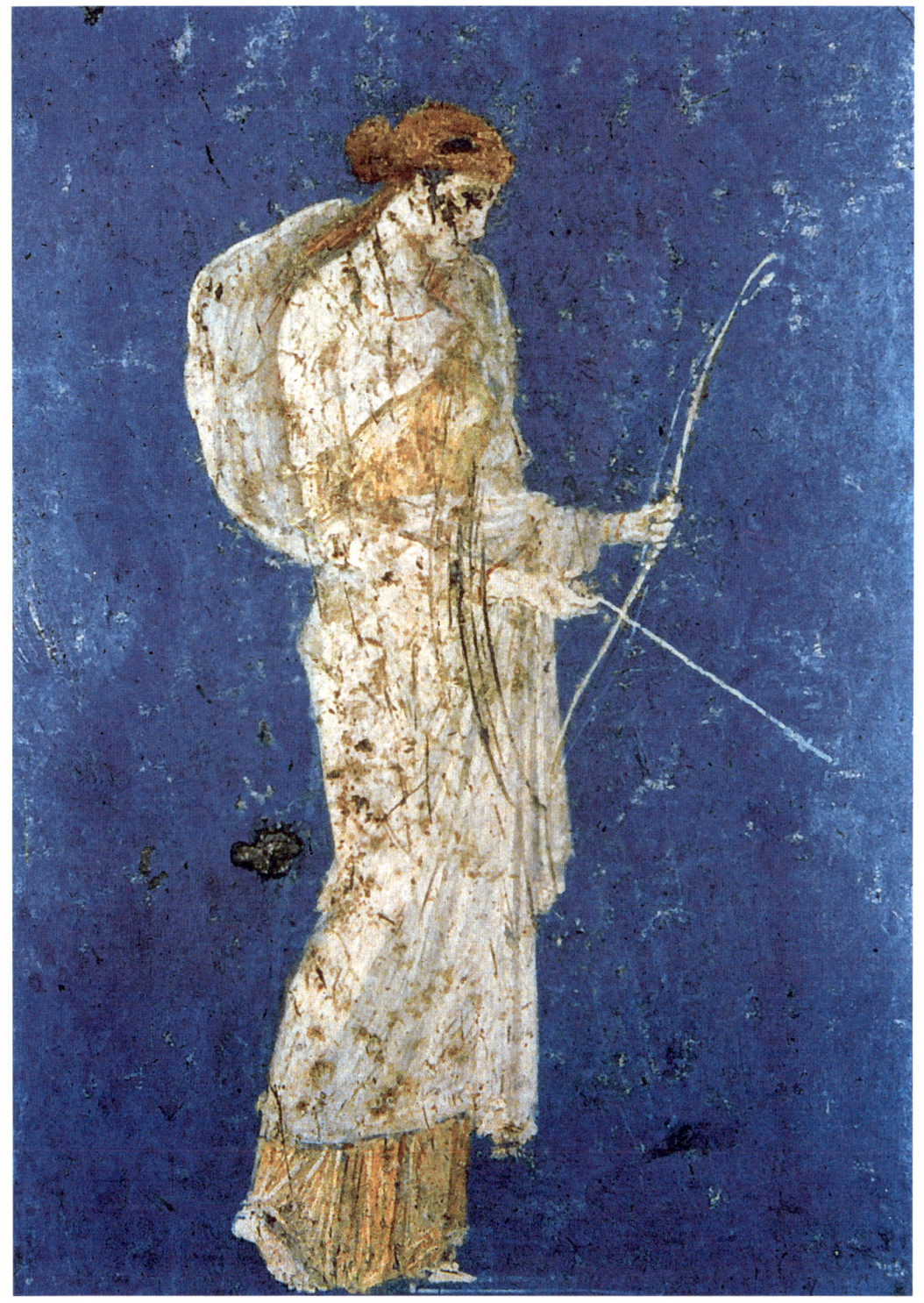

Mask of Xiuhtecuhtli

1400-1521

Death in Blue

In the Aztec Empire there was no major distinction between art and crafts, both developing an equally refined aesthetic in their decoration of secular and religious objects. The decorative masks typical of this civilisation were used during religious ceremonies and for funerary purposes.

What does this wooden mask covered with a mosaic of turquoises represent? Very probably the god of fire, Xiuhtecuhtli, whose name meant 'Turquoise God'. Yet some have suggested that it could be the sun deity Tonatiuh – the warts he traditionally has in Aztec iconography are symbolised here by the excrescences visible on the mask. Nevertheless, the first hypothesis seems more plausible. Especially since Xiuhtecuhtli's attribute is the butterfly and since many believe that the variations of blue on the mask's cheeks, chin and forehead allude to this.

The tonal variations of the stones are precise, creating contrasts between the contours of the face to give it a more realistic relief. The mother-of-pearl eyes and teeth starkly contrast with the intricate turquoise mosaic. The Aztecs revered turquoise, regarding it as synonymous with the power of life and the gods. Yet the person who wore this mask during a religious ritual had to detach himself from any such notion because he knew he would be sacrificed after the ceremony!

Turquoise mask,
said to be Xiuhtecuhtli
1400-1521
Wood, mother-of-pearl and
turquoise mosaic
British Museum, London

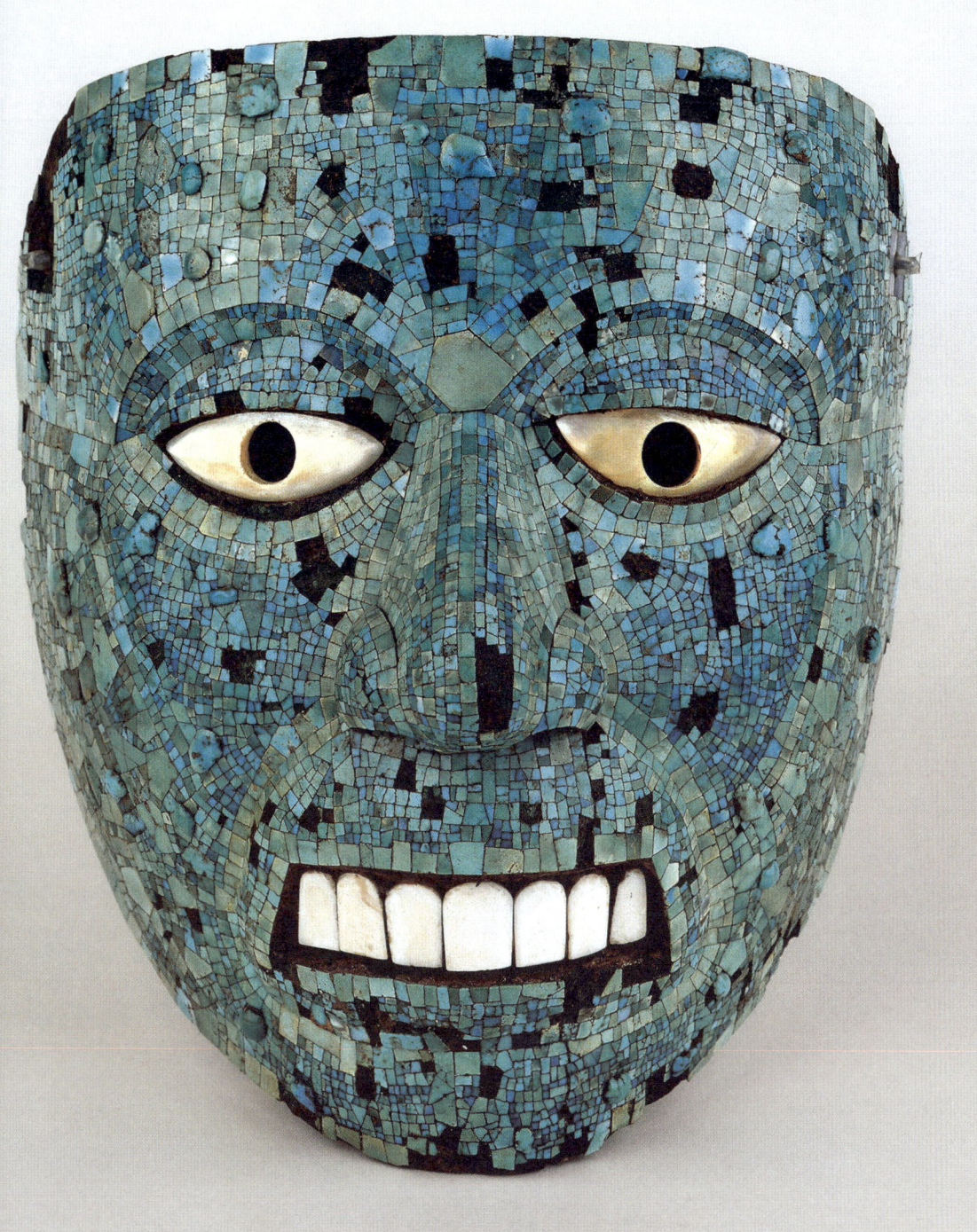

The Drapers' Window

ca. 1460

Suger Blue

Around 1140 Abbot Suger directed the reconstruction of the abbey church of Saint-Denis. He wanted light and he wanted colour, so stained-glass painters created 'Saint-Denis blue' (or 'Suger blue') for him. They took their formula with them from site to site, to Vendôme, Chartres, Le Mans etc., where it became 'Chartres blue', 'Le Mans blue', and so on.

Colouring Stained Glass

In the Middle Ages stained glass was often made with a fragile and therefore thick potassic glass. To colour it, artisans introduced metallic oxides into the molten paste: for blue, cobalt or safre; for red, copper oxide; for green, iron; for yellow, manganese

A Spiritual Tribute

At the beginning of the 12th century the Basilica of Saint-Denis and Chartres and Le Mans cathedrals pioneered the use of blue in their stained glass. It became known as 'Suger blue', after the the abbot who initiated work on the basilica.

Throughout the Middle Ages churches and cathedrals were embellished with blue stained glass in order to change the daylight filtering through into a metaphysical illumination for worshippers. Usually used decoratively and as a ground, blue was also the preferred colour for the mantle of the Virgin Mary.

In the collegiate church of Notre-Dame at Semur-en-Auxois, whose construction began in 1225, several stained-glass windows are dedicated to the butchers' and drapers' guilds. The window representing the drapers, dating from the mid 15th century and comprising eight panels, is in the Saint-Blaise Chapel, named after the brotherhood's patron saint. The different stages in the draper's trade, from the shearing of sheep for their wool to cutting the fabric, are depicted simply and accurately. Here the wool is being beaten to soften it.

Interestingly, it was the master glaziers who decided that the fabric on which the drapers are shown working should be blue. This was obviously a purely aesthetic choice, for even though blue garments existed in the Middle Ages thanks to indigo dyes, they rarely had such a rich colour. If they did, they were reserved for the aristocracy. Dyeing is the very last stage in the making of cloth, so there was no reason for it to be blue in the step pictured here. But by including this colour in the stained glass the artists were emphasising its mystical message and also imbuing the drapers' guild with a certain nobility.

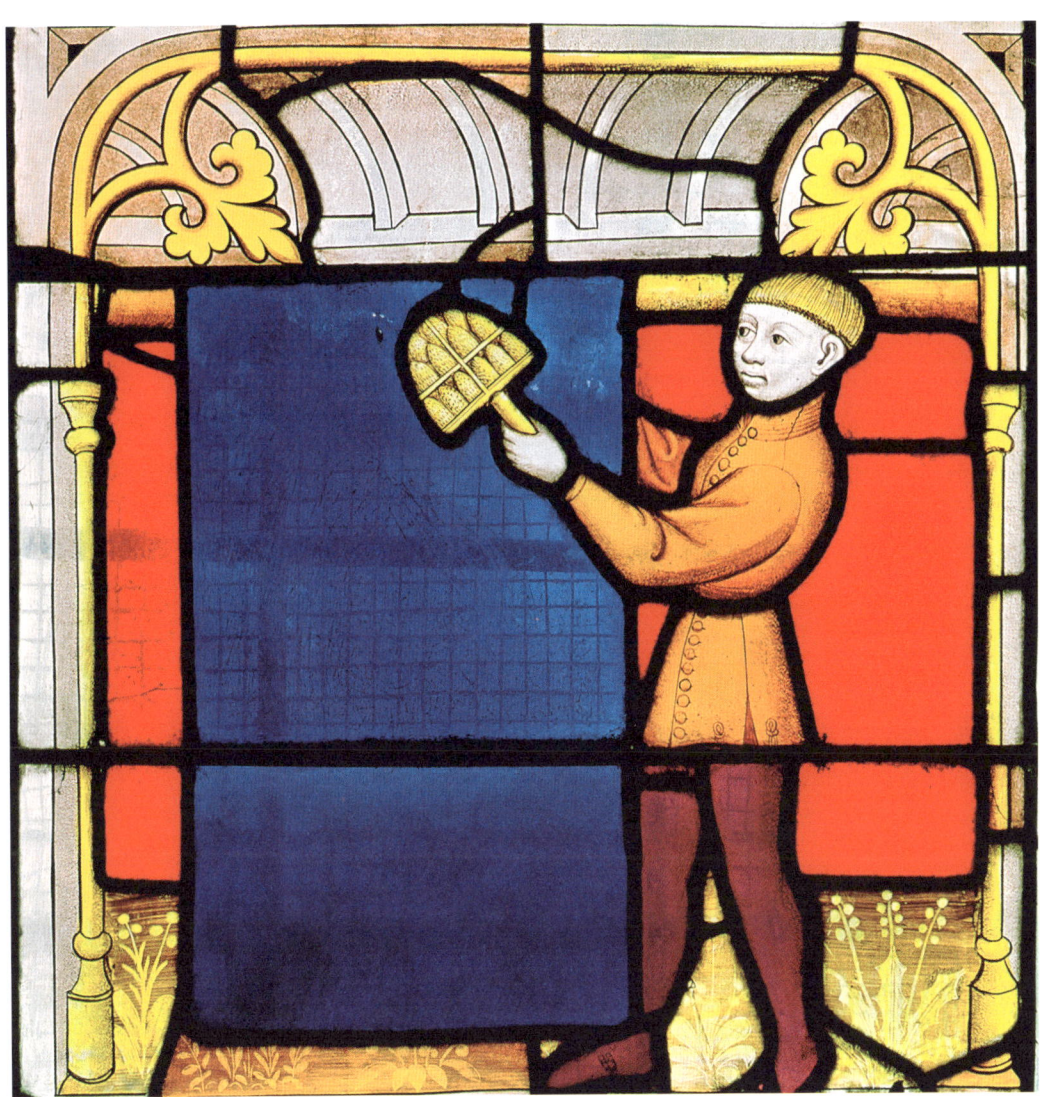

The Drapers' Window
ca. 1460
Stained glass
Collégiale Notre-Dame, Semur-en-Auxois

Iznik tile

1525–50

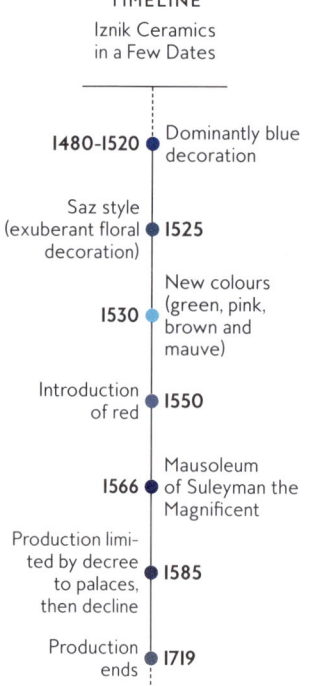

TIMELINE

Iznik Ceramics
in a Few Dates

1480-1520	Dominantly blue decoration
Saz style (exuberant floral decoration)	1525
1530	New colours (green, pink, brown and mauve)
Introduction of red	1550
1566	Mausoleum of Suleyman the Magnificent
Production limited by decree to palaces, then decline	1585
Production ends	1719

Blue Interiors

Ottoman aristocrats were art lovers and also great collectors of the so-called 'blue and white' porcelain produced during the Ming dynasty in China. This taste inspired ceramics workshops in the town of Iznik in present-day Turkey.

Beginning in the late 15th century artisans produced ceramics with painted decoration composed of a very white, smooth, hard siliceous paste made up of 80 % silica, 20 % clay and degreasing agents. Motifs in cobalt blue were painted on the white tile then coated with a shiny glaze. Their themes were often floral, reproducing the plant forms of the Islamic repertoire but also greatly influenced by Chinese art.

From the late 1520s onwards, turquoise blue was combined with cobalt blue, and green was introduced in the 1530s, when this tile was produced. Alongside traditional decorative pieces and crockery, in the mid 16th century Iznik began producing tiles. Their refined, ornate motifs graced religious monuments and the palaces of the Ottoman Empire.

One has to imagine these tiles set in monumental ensembles to create stylised landscapes catering to the Ottoman elite's passion for horticulture and transposing their luxuriant gardens into interior décor. And why was blue so omnipresent? The Far-Eastern influence is undeniable and reflects the Asian trade that spread to Europe. But there is also the exaltation of blue in an environment of clay and ochre-coloured architecture. The contrast is magnificent. But in the end everything is merely a matter of taste.

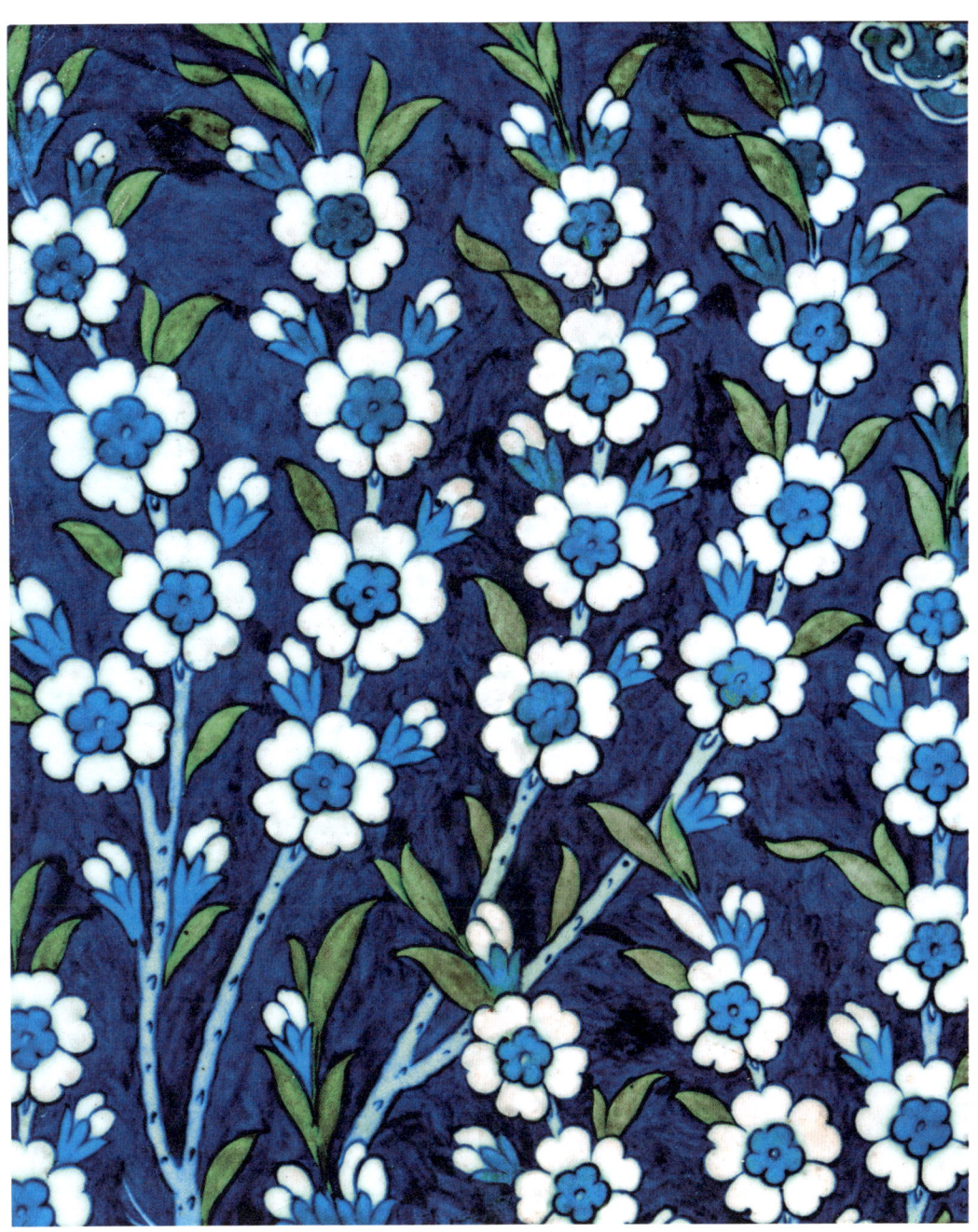

Wall tile
1525–50
Iznik ceramic with underglaze decoration
Victoria and Albert Museum, London

The Opening of the Fifth Seal

1614

An Apocalyptic Vision

Born in Crete, Domínikos Theotokópoulos, known as El Greco, trained as an icon painter. When he travelled to Italy in 1570 he discovered Michelangelo and his treatment of the human body. He expressed this influence in a Mannerist style which reached its peak after he settled in Spain.

The Opening of the Fifth Seal is one of the three altarpieces El Greco painted for the church of the Saint John the Baptist Hospital in Toledo. It depicts a passage from the Book of Revelations. Inspired by intense religious fervour, the painter rendered biblical scenes in a novel, disconcerting manner, subjecting the expressions and poses of the figures, colour and light to his spirituality.

In the left foreground Saint John is raising his arms to the heavens in an ecstatic gesture. Encouraged by the naked figures of martyrs demanding vengeance and therefore the destruction of the world, he seems to be imploring the thundery sky to swallow up the world in its frenzied swirling motion.

The dazzling light plays a major role in this manifestation of disorder, as does the colourful drapery contrasting with the deathly white skin tones. The elongated, unnatural, disturbingly monumental figures convey a vertical, spiritual momentum. El Greco's forms are almost abstract and only the vivid colours stabilise our vision of the scene. Colour alone catches the light in a world that the artist, contrary to tradition, has plunged into darkness. Not even religion has been spared. El Greco is daring to show us that where there is light there is also darkness.

But there is the light reflected by John's shimmering blue garment, a Marian blue counterbalancing the tension of the composition's swirling motion, a brilliant blue of hope.

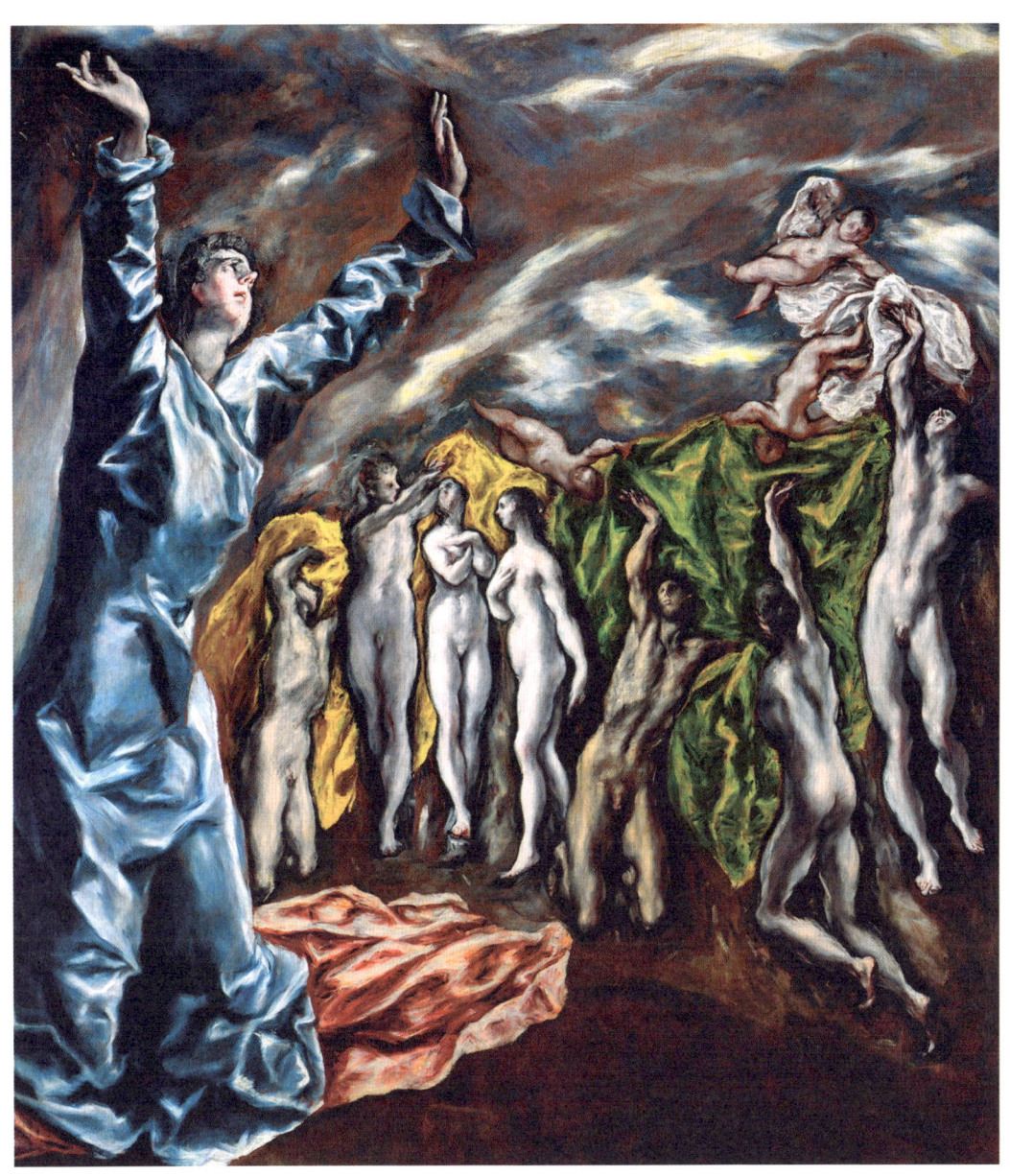

The Opening of the Fifth Seal
Domínikos Theotokópoulos,
known as El Greco (1541–1614)
1614
Oil on canvas
The Metropolitan Museum of Art, New York

73

Marie-Henriette Berthelot de Pléneuf

1739

A Name, a Colour

Jean-Marc Nattier is not alone in having his name associated with a colour. There is Klein blue, Veronese green, Majorelle blue, Monory blue, Soulages ultrablack, and in the fashion world there are Schiaparelli's shocking pink and Lanvin blue.

Posterity in a Blue

During the reign of Louis XV, when Jean-Marc Nattier was a renowned portraitist at court, painting embraced the rococo aesthetic in works privileging intimate, often bucolic scenes.

Although this is a portrait of an aristocrat, Marie-Henriette Berthelot de Pléneuf is not portrayed realistically. In the taste of the time, Nattier sought to portray his subjects in an idealised manner. And to add a touch of fantasy, he specialised in allegorical portraits.

Here his model is posing as a personification of water, then a very popular mythological theme. The large jar spouting water beneath her right arm, symbolising a spring, explicitly supports this allegory. There are also aquatic reeds on her left.

But above all it is the painter's colours that further link the picture with the theme of water. The backdrop is composed of nuances ranging from silver blue to green. The figure, wearing a pale-coloured dress, her almost translucent skin heightened only with touches of red on her cheeks and lips, has a virginal aura about it. She is theatrically wrapped in brilliant blue drapery that enhances not only the majesty of her portrayal but also the aquatic metaphor which seems to be literally engulfing her.

Nattier has often been criticised for the lack of psychology in his portraits. Nevertheless, his name passed to posterity when in the 20th century the luminous blue in which he was so fond of draping his female subjects became known as 'Nattier blue'.

Marie-Henriette Berthelot de Pléneuf
Jean-Marc Nattier (1685-1766)
1739
Oil on canvas
National Museum of Western Art, Tokyo

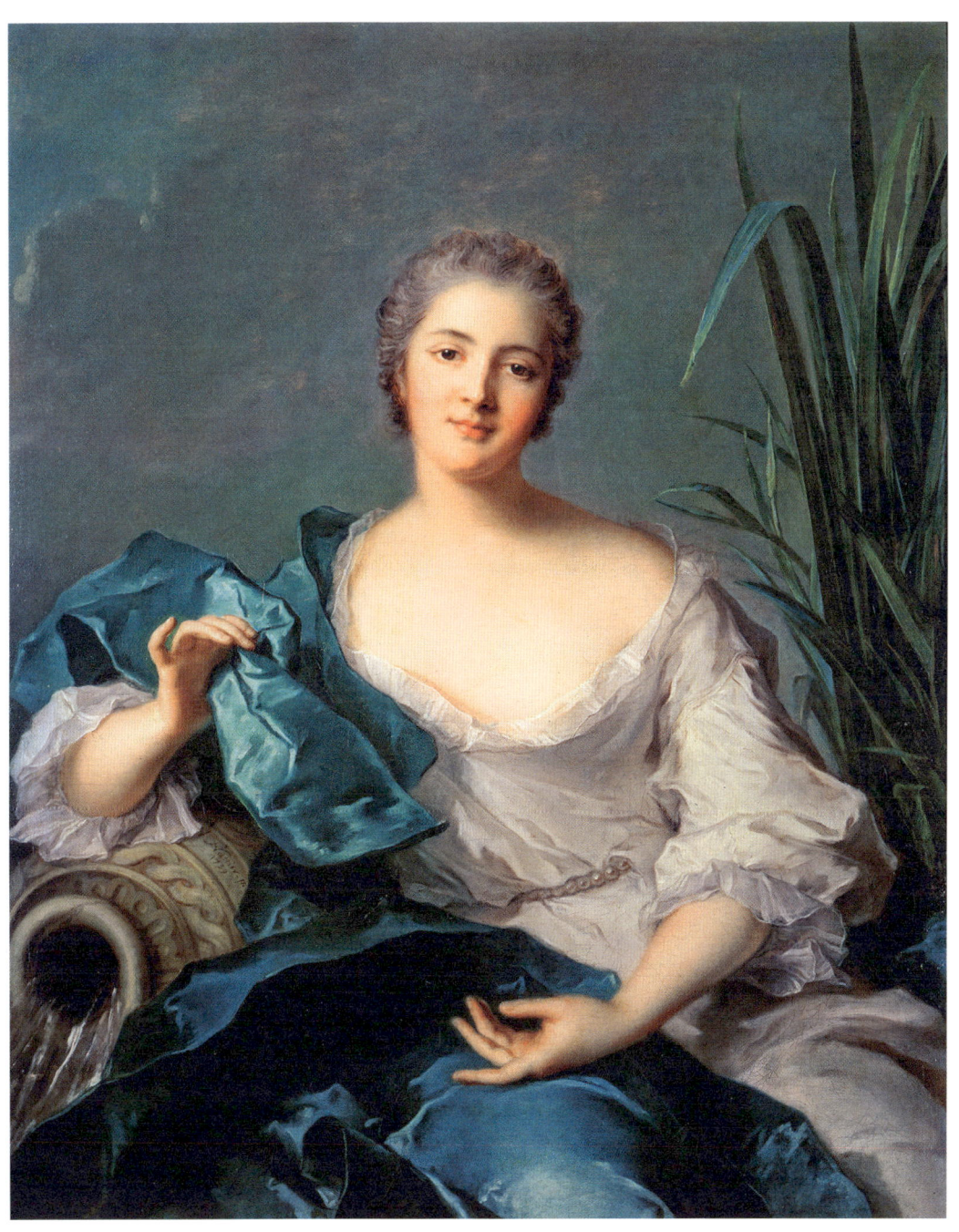

The Monk by the Sea

1808–10

An Unromantic Romanticism

Romanticism was a movement in art that spread throughout Europe between 1780 and 1850. A far cry from candlelit dinners and rose petals, it sought to express states of mind often shrouded in mystery and melancholy, sometimes depicting morbid, dreamlike states and visions of the past, the infinite and the void.

A German Blue

Around 1704, intending to create red as he routinely did, the chemist Johann Jacob Diesbach made a mistake in his combination of iron sulphate and potassium and produced an intense blue colour. His discovery became known as Prussian blue. His formula was published by the Englishman John Woodward in 1724 and marketed beginning in the 1750s.

An Inner Dialogue

A Romantic par excellence, Caspar David Friedrich reinstated landscape at the heart of pictorial reflection. In _The Monk by the Sea_ he transformed it into a means of introspection.

His audacity here lies in the fact that in this painting there is apparently nothing to see. We are immediately struck by the sky occupying three quarters of the picture. Everything else has become almost anecdotal: the dark sea dotted with white foam and the monk half turned away from us on a barren stretch of dune.

This is a large picture, a metre high and two metres wide, so imagine yourself in front of it, gazing into the infinite space that Friedrich is intent on depicting. He has done away with all borders, limits and narrative elements to leave only a boundless landscape.

The landscape has become a pretext for meditation. The vaporous blue sky instills calm yet is not devoid of melancholy, accentuated by the tiny, solitary figure facing the vastness of the world. Yet the monk is not inviting us to contemplate this grandiose sight. He is lost in his own thoughts, unaware of us. It is the sky alone, not his human presence, that immerses us in the picture.

What is Friedrich trying to say here? Is he using the vastness of the sky to evoke a mystical communion, the sublime - he did after all choose a monk as the picture's sole protagonist? Or was he trying to demonstrate man's insignificance faced with the grandeur of creation?

The Monk by the Sea
Caspar David Friedrich
(1774–1840)
1808–10
Oil on canvas
Alte Nationalgalerie, Berlin

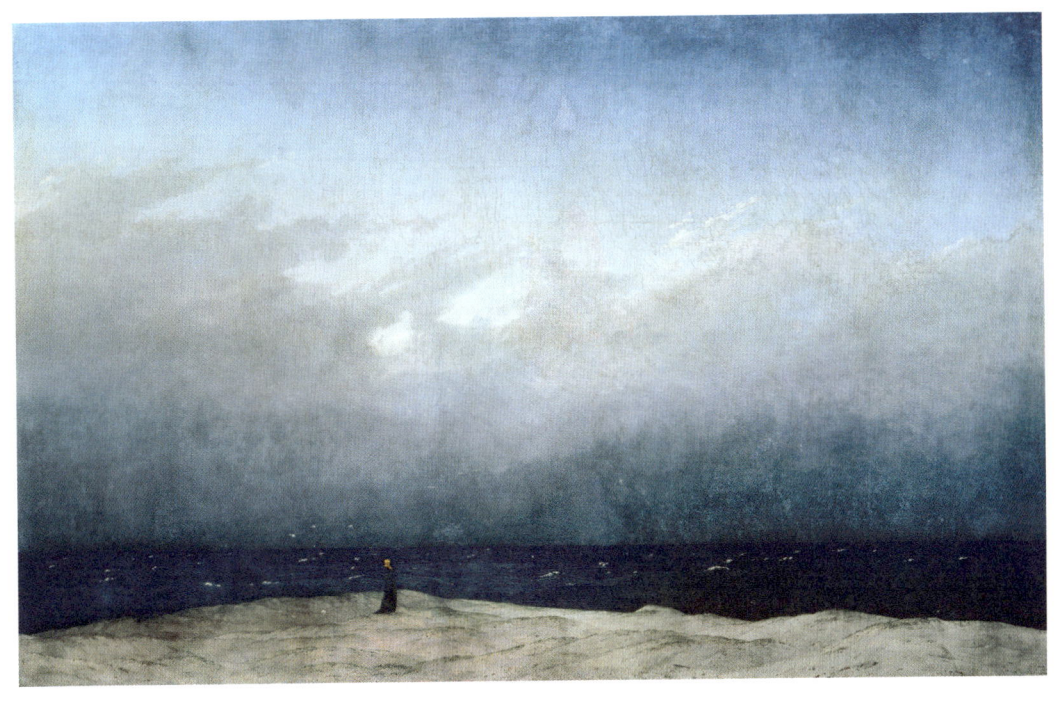

'Free man, you will always cherish the sea!
The sea is your mirror; you contemplate your soul
In the infinite unrolling of its billows;
Your mind is an abyss that is no less bitter'.

Charles Baudelaire, 'L'Homme et la mer', *Les Fleurs du mal*

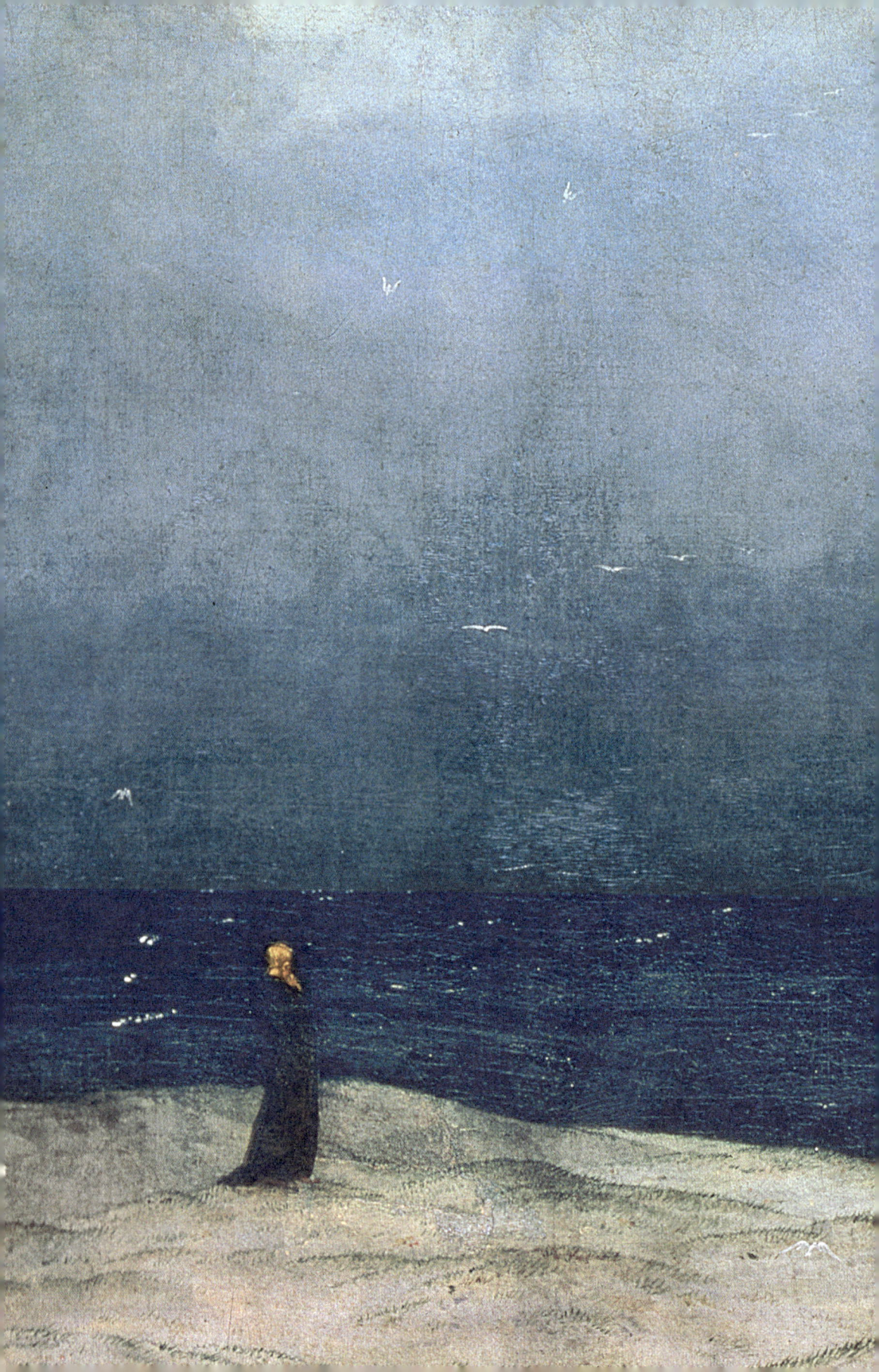

Nocturne in Blue and Silver: Chelsea

1871

Night Music

The Irish composer John Field is credited with developing the musical form of the nocturne in the mid 19th century, previously tunes to be performed in the open air. Nocturnes are classical compositions, slow in tempo except for their middle section. They became emblematic of the Romantic movement: Frédéric Chopin composed the most famous ones.

TIMELINE

Whistler Nocturnes

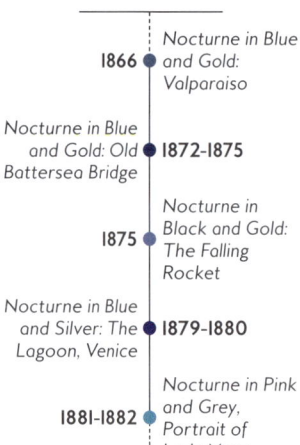

1866 — Nocturne in Blue and Gold: Valparaiso

Nocturne in Blue and Gold: Old Battersea Bridge — **1872-1875**

1875 — Nocturne in Black and Gold: The Falling Rocket

Nocturne in Blue and Silver: The Lagoon, Venice — **1879-1880**

1881-1882 — Nocturne in Pink and Grey, Portrait of Lady Meux

The City by Night

Travelling up the Thames one summer evening, Whistler was struck by the gleaming water as the sun was setting. He hurried to his studio and began painting this evanescent scene.

A nocturnal riverscape, but a very luminous one! And hardly surprising that Whistler saw silver in his blue. He diluted his paint as if it were watercolour to create vaporous transparent effects scattered with reflections and dots of light. Water and sky have become one in the mist over the river. But he is also delicately evoking night falling over the city.

Yet human activity is still present. Across the river we can see the district of Chelsea, and there is a lone fisherman in the foreground. Yet despite these presences, Whistler succeeded in capturing the scene's poetry and serenity in a single moment – a calm evoking Japanese art, to which Whistler is also paying tribute here by including his favourite signature in the middle at the bottom.

It was not Whistler who titled the picture *Nocturne* but Frederick Leyland, a shipowner, in reference to the musical genre. This pleased the artist because it epitomised the composition's equilibrium, and like a melody the painting awakens emotions and the sense of mystery that only the night can.

'Dusk began to sweep over the sea.
And the sky slowly darkened'.

Marguerite Duras

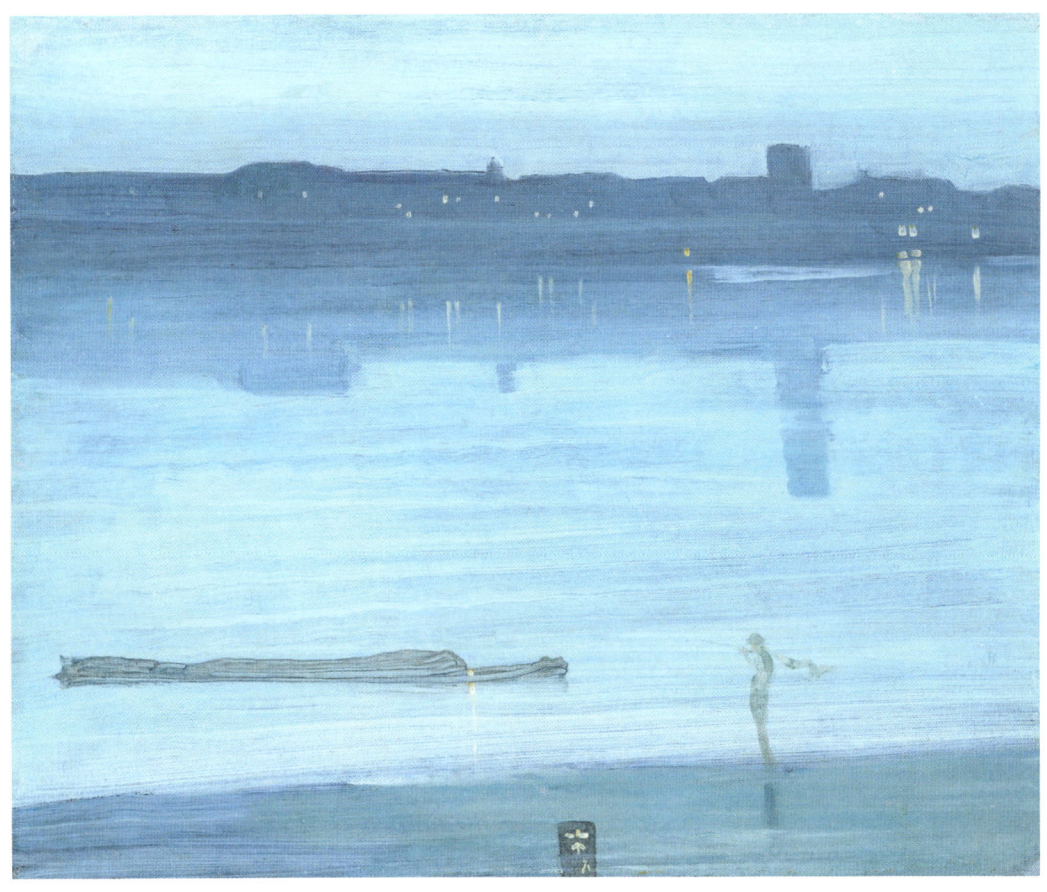

Nocturne in Blue and Silver: Chelsea
James McNeill Whistler (1834–1903)
1871
Oil on wood
Tate Collection, London

The Golden Cell

1892

What Do We Dream of?

In the 1890s Odilon Redon introduced colour into his work, until then principally consisting of charcoal drawings and lithographs emphasising the black line.

Colour enabled Redon to further impregnate his work with a dreamlike atmosphere. With his esoteric approach to existence and fondness for exploring the soul and the human mind, he mingled illusion and reality in works linking him to the Symbolist movement and establishing him as a precursor of Surrealism.

When *The Golden Cell* was shown for the first time at Paul Durand-Ruel's Paris gallery in 1894, it baffled the public. The critic Camille Mauclair wrote: 'I fail to understand the relationship between the colours and the drawing: Why blues here and golds there?' And when the writer Tolstoy saw the picture he wondered whether it was really art.

There are many women depicted in profile in Redon's work. They often seem like priestesses or deities. With her cobalt blue face evoking the spiritual world, the woman seen here resembles a Byzantine icon or a Madonna, her holiness emphasised by a kind of gold halo.

Redon was fond of depicting his subjects with closed eyes. There was a certain morbid symbolism in this, but it evoked above all the world of sleep and dreams. The mysticism conveyed here is less a religious element than an expression of our inner world. Where do our thoughts go when we close our eyes?

Paul Durand-Ruel

The son of Parisian art dealers, Durand-Ruel promoted a new generation of painters rejecting official art. He signed exclusive contracts with Camille Corot and Jean-François Millet and aided Gustave Courbet, Édouard Manet, Claude Monet, Camille Pissarro and Auguste Renoir.

The Blue Challenge

In 1799 the French Interior Minister commissioned the chemist Louis Jacques Thénard to produce a less costly blue. Thénard heated cobalt salts with alumine to obtain a blue marketed as 'Thénard blue'. In 1828 Jean-Baptiste Guimet discovered an even less expensive synthetic ultramarine.

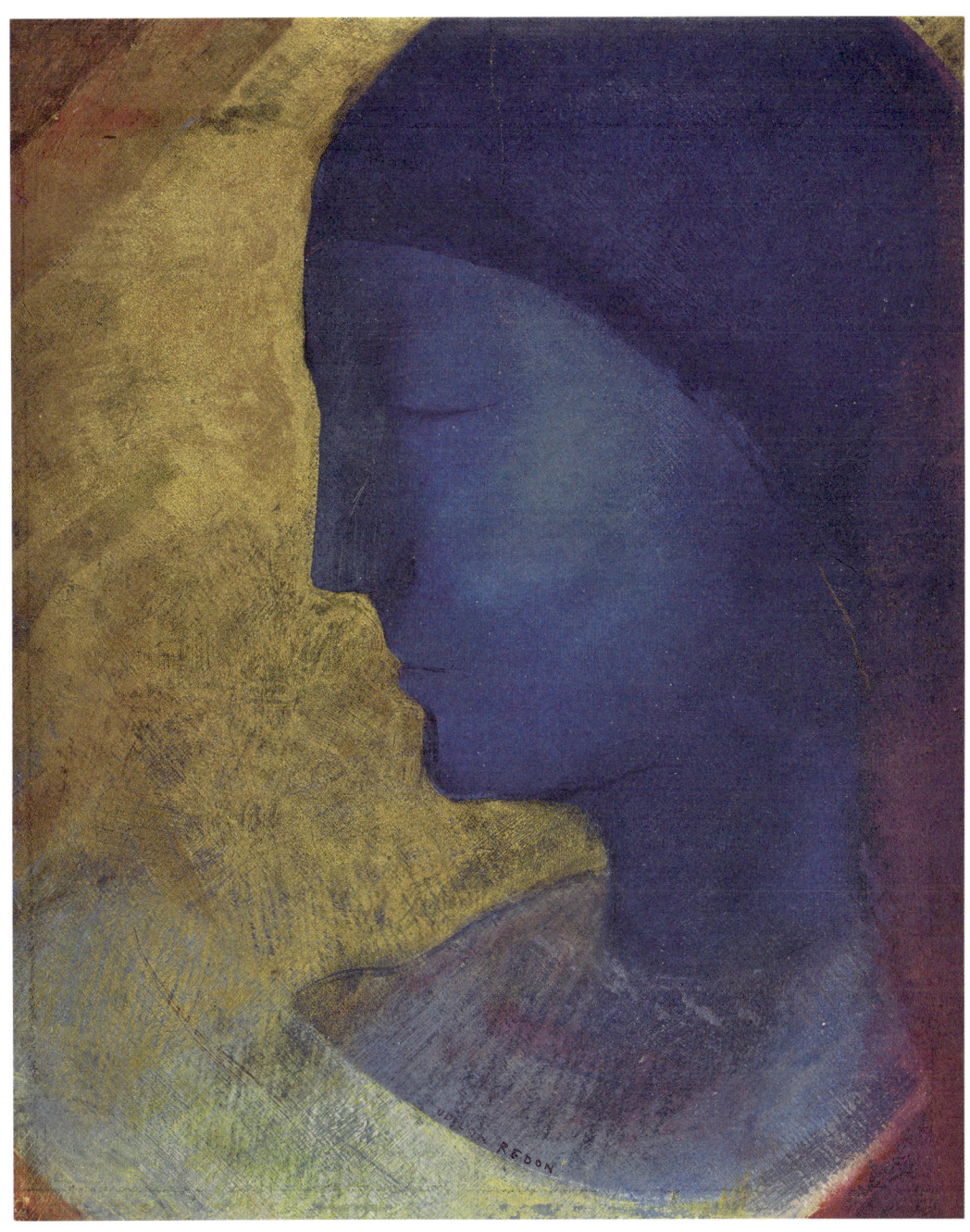

The Golden Cell
Odilon Redon (1840–1916)
1892
Pastel and oil on paper
British Museum, London

Manhattan Bridge

1922

How Does It Work?

A sheet of opaque white paper, or negative, is coated with a solution of chemicals (ferric ammonium citrate and potassium ferricyanide), then dried in complete darkness. When it is exposed to light in a photograph the composition of iron salts changes. The paper or negative is then rinsed with cold water and dried. During drying the parts of the image exposed to light turn blue.

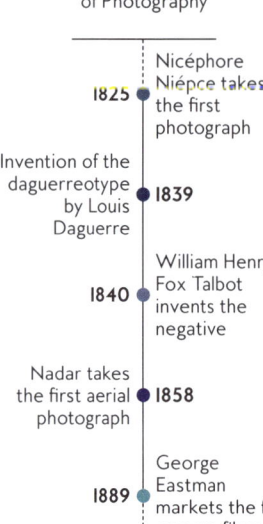

TIMELINE

The Beginnings of Photography

1825 Nicéphore Niépce takes the first photograph

Invention of the daguerreotype by Louis Daguerre **1839**

1840 William Henry Fox Talbot invents the negative

Nadar takes the first aerial photograph **1858**

1889 George Eastman markets the first camera films

The Vertiginous Growth of a City

In 1842 the English chemist John Frederick William Herschel invented a photographic process producing an intense blue print called a cyanotype.

Hershel's discovery had little initial success because the unnatural appearance of these prints was unsuited to photographers seeking realism in their work. But it was an excellent medium for such industrial uses as the duplication of architectural plans and technical drawings ('blueprints'). The cyanotype is very resistant to light, simple to use and inexpensive.

At the end of the 19th century the technique became popular with amateur photographers, allowing them to produce family albums cheaply. And the Pictorialists, proponents of the international style that dominated photography from 1890 to around 1914 and whose concerns were primarily aesthetic, rediscovered its delicate, poetic qualities.

Was it this that motivated Eugene de Salignac's use of the process? In his work as photographer for New York's Department of Bridges starting in 1903, he took numerous photographs documenting the department's work and in doing so provided us with admirable testimony to the city's explosive growth.

This is true of this view of the Manhattan Bridge. It is difficult to tell whether de Salignac's use of the cyanotype was an artistic choice or merely a practical one. Having used this technique for many years, was he aware of the sentimental significance of his images? The omnipresence of blue accentuates the ambient atmosphere, lending a morose tinge to an already grey, misty day. Was he unconsciously revealing the melancholy looming behind the vertiginous growth of modernity?

'I express the wish that photography,
instead of falling into the domain of industry
and commerce, enters that of art'.

Gustave Le Gray

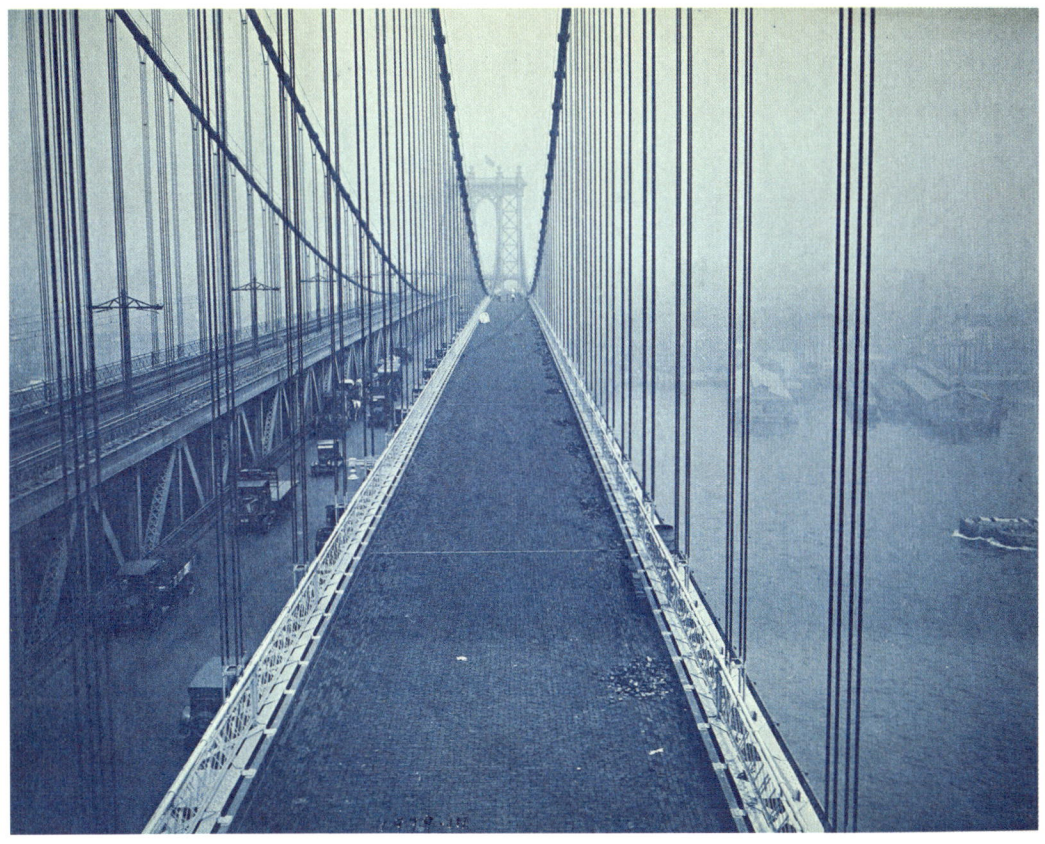

Manhattan Bridge
Eugene de Salignac (1861-1943)
1922
Cyanotype
Worcester Art Museum

Street Decked with American Banners

ca. 1930

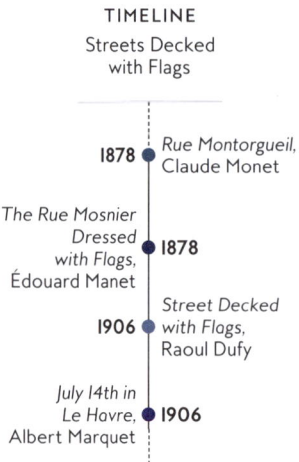

TIMELINE
Streets Decked
with Flags

1878 *Rue Montorgueil,*
Claude Monet

The Rue Mosnier
Dressed
with Flags, **1878**
Édouard Manet

Street Decked
1906 *with Flags,*
Raoul Dufy

July 14th in
Le Havre, **1906**
Albert Marquet

Patriotisms

Raoul Dufy preferred the festive aspect of the street and he was not alone. This joyful, patriotic subject was frequently captured in the late 19th century and even more so after the horrors of the First World War.

What could be more heartening than a street decked with flags and banners? What more wonderful sight than the city draped in vivid colours? For Dufy it was also a symbol of modernity, because a street decked with flags was a pretext for depicting crowds and urban architecture. This painting was used as the poster for the Salon des artistes décorateurs in 1939, whose theme was the street. It is still unclear whether the picture was painted specifically for this poster.

Raoul Dufy often painted this subject because it perfectly suited his Fauvist style. Here the brightly coloured banners and their simplified geometric forms contrast with the more neutral tones of the city and the barely sketched-in lines of the figures. It is as if these banners were swallowing up everything, and to accentuate this effect he deliberately allowed the blue of the building to flood into the street and engulf the silhouettes of passers-by. There is little concern for realism here, it is the dominance of this patriotic blue that is the picture's prime subject.

One can see this image uniting the French and American flags as a premonition of an indispensable alliance to come. In 1946 the writer and art collector Gertrude Stein, who did much to promote the work of Cézanne, Picasso and Matisse, wrote: 'Raoul Dufy is pleasure'. She could also have written 'Raoul Dufy is an antidote'.

'There are only two things to do with a flag, brandish it at arm's length or passionately press it to one's heart'.

Paul Claudel

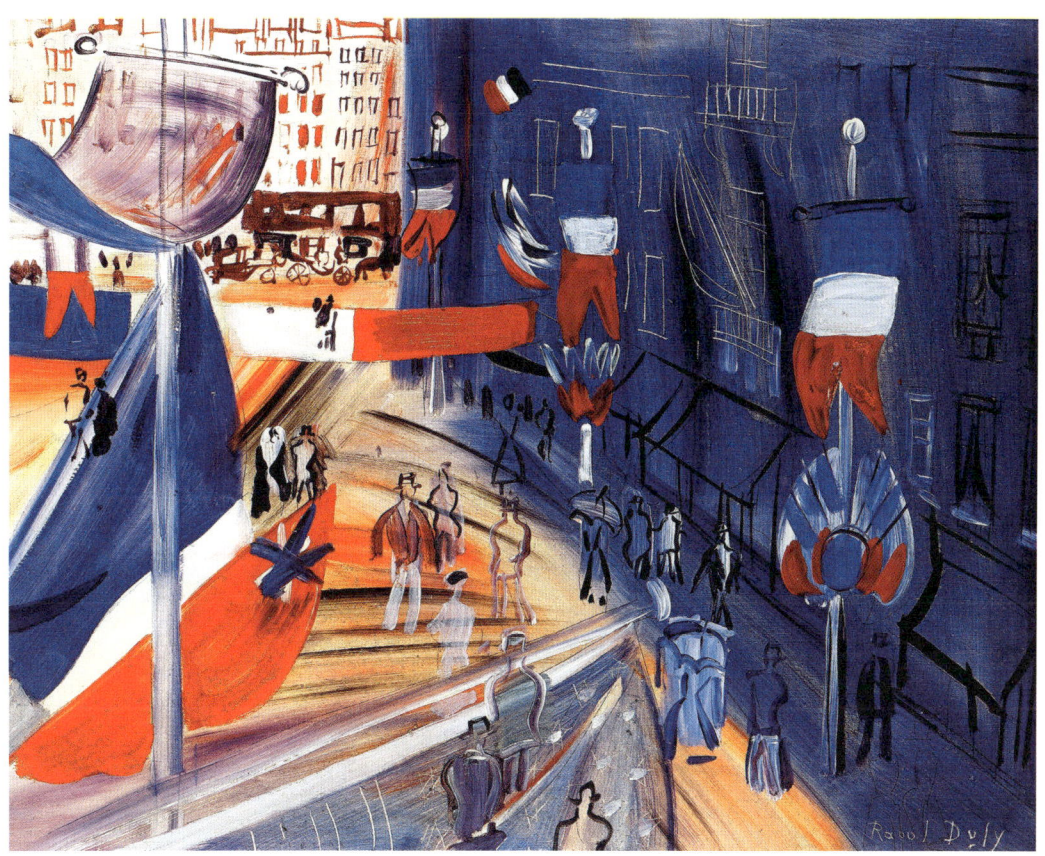

Street Decked with American Banners
Raoul Dufy (1877–1953)
ca. 1930
Oil on cardboard
Private collection

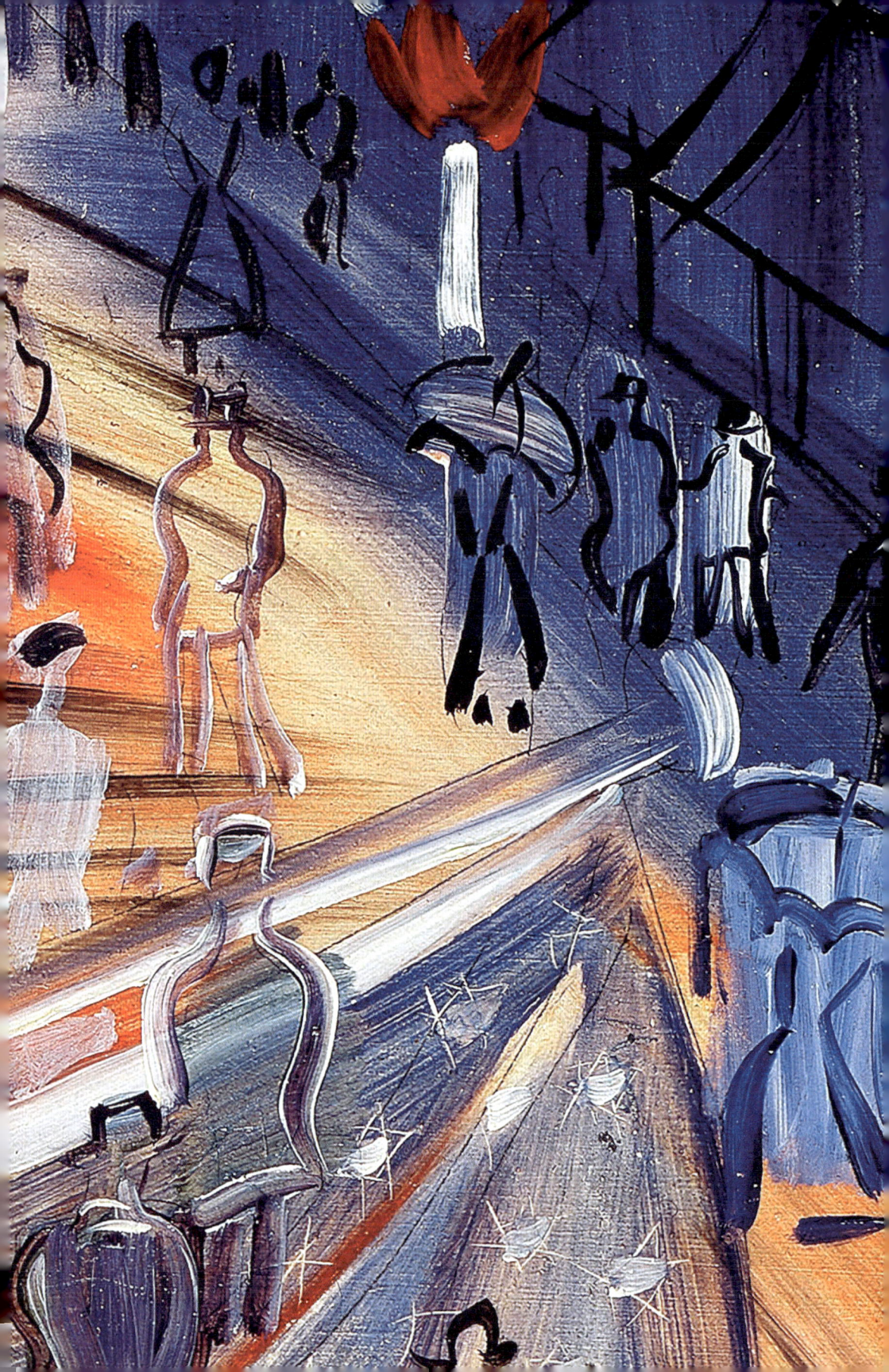

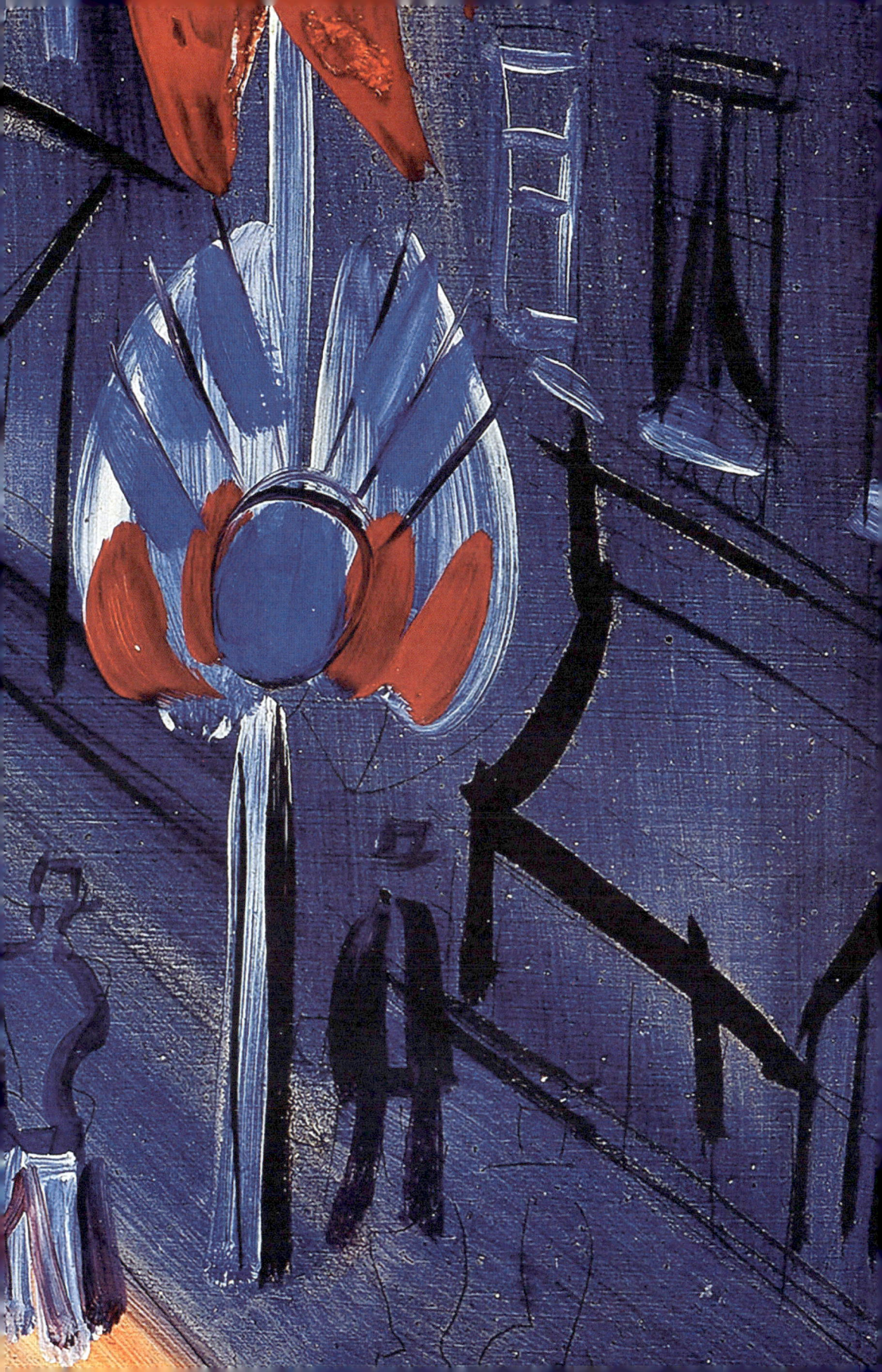

Sky Blue

1940

Colours and Spirituality

In his theoretical work *Concerning the Spiritual in Art*, published in 1911, Kandinsky emphasised the psychological effect of colours on the soul. He considered blue to be a celestial colour evoking profound calm. He adds that a blue surface produces a sensation of distance, in contrast to yellow surfaces, which give the impression of being closer to us.

Life in Blue

In 1940, during the German Occupation, Wassily Kandinsky and his wife were forced to live a secluded life in their apartment in Neuilly-sur-Seine. Yet despite these morose circumstances, he produced this whimsical, optimistic work.

A recent inspiration for him were the medieval tapestries he had discovered in Paris, and the combinations of colours in this painting are indeed reminiscent of textile patchworks.

In these strange creatures one cannot help but see a butterfly, a fish and even a giraffe's head. But one would be wasting one's time, for there is nothing real about these figures. They have more to do with scientific imagery, such as cells viewed through a microscope. Kandinsky has metamorphosed these entities into a disparate ensemble of colourful new beings, into an ode to life at a time when death was everywhere.

The backdrop for this celebration of existence at its purest is a celestial blue echoing the blue sky he could see from his studio window, a link with an atmosphere far from earthly horrors. And if Kandinsky named this picture after that blue sky it was because it mattered so much to him.

In this work, comparable to those of Miró, Kandinsky is offering us a magical spectacle, a festive dance that transports us into a dreamlike, playful world he created in order to forget a world at war.

Sky Blue
Wassily Kandinsky (1866–1944)
1940
Oil on canvas
Musée national d'Art moderne,
Centre Pompidou, Paris

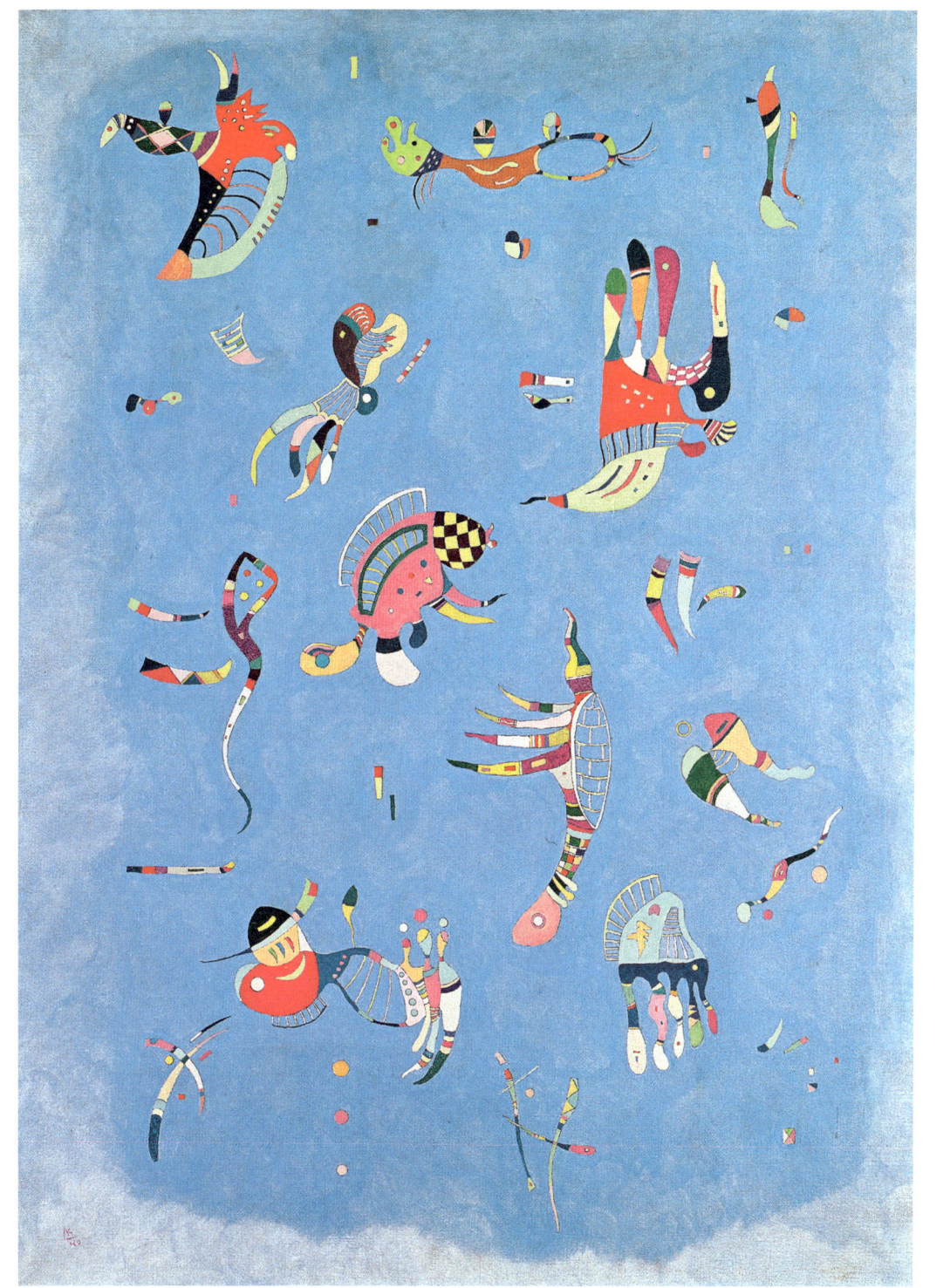

Sea Watchers

1952

Seaside Blues

A day at the seaside is usually associated with pleasure and carefree holidays, but for Edward Hopper it can have gruelling, melancholy overtones.

A man and a woman sit motionlessly on a bench in front of their beach house, gazing at the sea without the slightest visible emotion. The only movement is the linen flapping in the wind on the clothesline. Everything is flat, oppressively horizontal.

The poses of the two figures seem opposed. The woman is leaning back, as though resigned to her married existence, while the man leans slightly forward. He seems to be tempted by some impulse, but his slightly hunched back indicates that this impetus has now gone. He wants to but will not.

And suddenly this sunny day becomes overcast, even sad. The blue of the sky and sea invading the scene and also the shadow of the house have become sullen threats. Instead of gazing at the immensity of the blue sea, the man is now trapped in that blue. It is no longer a blue of freedom but of sadness. Two figures, each with his own torments, no longer enchanted by the radiant blue sky.

Divergences

In Hopper's pictures, couples are often caught in an overwhelming silence heightened by their seemingly unconnected figures.

1932: *Room in New York*

1952: *Hotel by a Railroad*

1959: *Excursion Into Philosophy*

1960: *Second Story Sunlight*

From Blue to the Blues

Blue can sometimes be the colour of melancholy. And if 'the blues' originated in the songs black slaves sang in the cotton fields in the American south, it is because they were expressing their sadness and tribulations.

Sea Watchers
Edward Hopper (1882–1967)
1952
Oil on canvas
Private collection

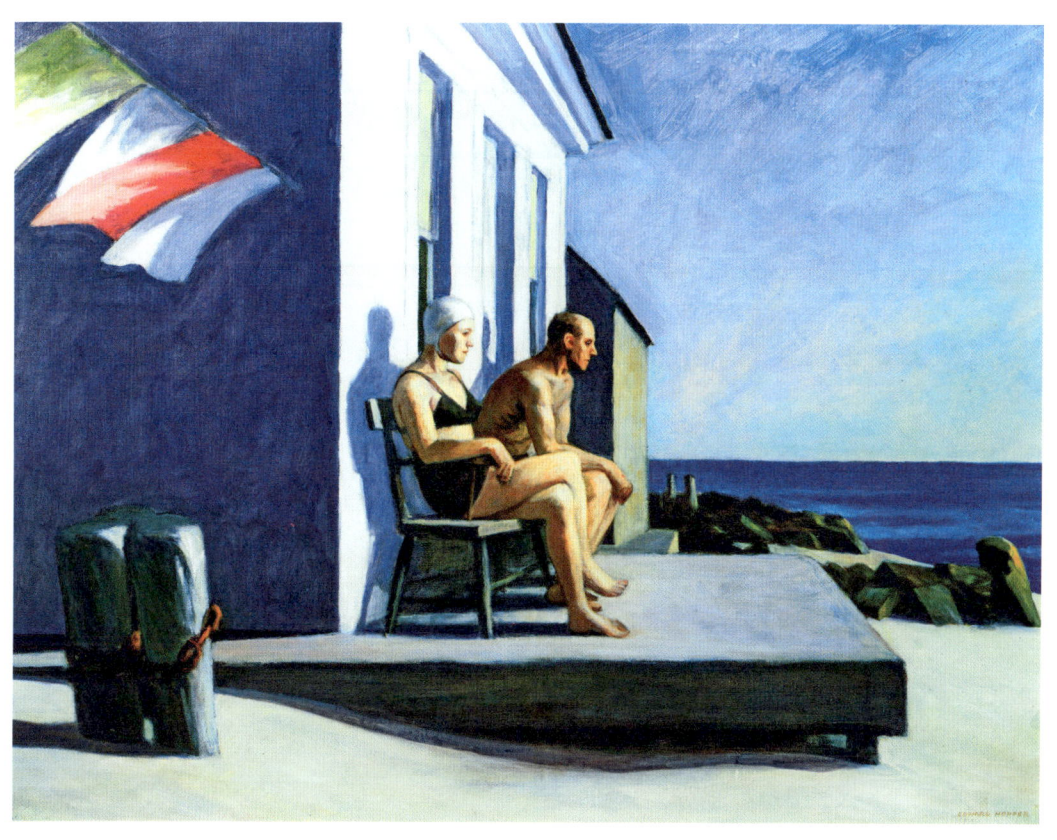

'Love does not consist of gazing at each other,
but in looking outward together in the same direction'.

Antoine de Saint-Exupéry

Provence Landscape

1953

Provençal Blue

In 1942 Nicolas de Staël abandoned classical representation to produce works in equilibrium between abstraction and figuration in which his impasto technique plays a major role.

In the early 1950s he moved to Provence, where he found a new creative impetus. Fascinated by the light and landscapes of the south of France, he painted pictures that marked a turning point in his life and work.

Daily he drew landscapes in his sketchbooks, endeavouring particularly to capture the changing light during the day. When he returned to his studio, he painted from memory and these sketches. For him it was not merely a matter of evoking a moment or place but above all his own powerful emotions; he was inspired not only by Provence but by a woman, an impossible love that had pitched him into a turmoil he transposed onto his canvases in thick impasto.

De Staël exulted in the southern sun with a palette of blues enabling him to mingle the nuances of sky and earth in a textural monochrome both dense and transparent. And despite this abstract treatment, the landscape remains palpable in its differing densities, perspective and trees. The various shades of blue unify them in a sublime glow. It is pure colour that provides the narration here. Only the light tones of the house stand out as a reminder of human presence.

TIMELINE
Skies and Seas
in Provence

1828 — *The Lighthouse at Marseille from the Sea*, J. M. W. Turner

The Port of Marseille in the Sunset, Félix Ziem — 1860

1878–1879 — *The Gulf of Marseille Seen from L'Estaque*, Paul Cézanne

The Starry Night, Vincent Van Gogh — 1888

1896 — *Pines Along the Shore*, Henri-Edmond Cross

'Blue recalls at most the sea and the sky,
that which is most abstract in tangible and visible nature'.

Yves Klein

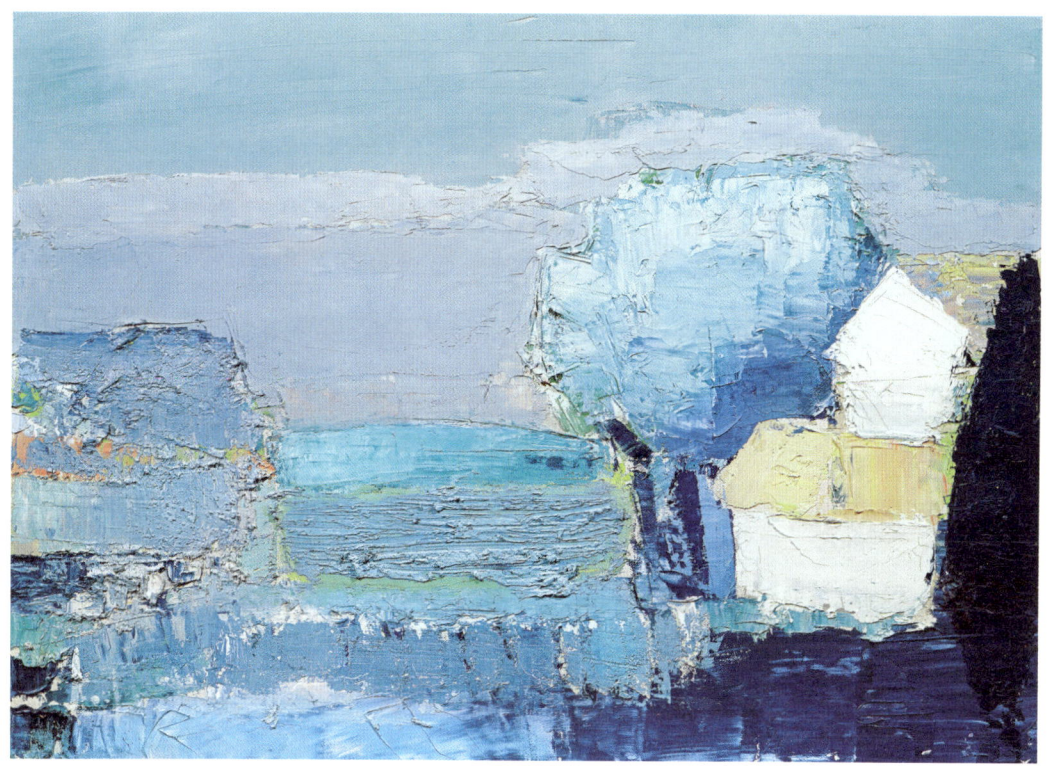

Provence Landscape
Nicolas de Staël (1914–55)
1953
Oil on canvas
Museo Thyssen-Bornemisza, Madrid

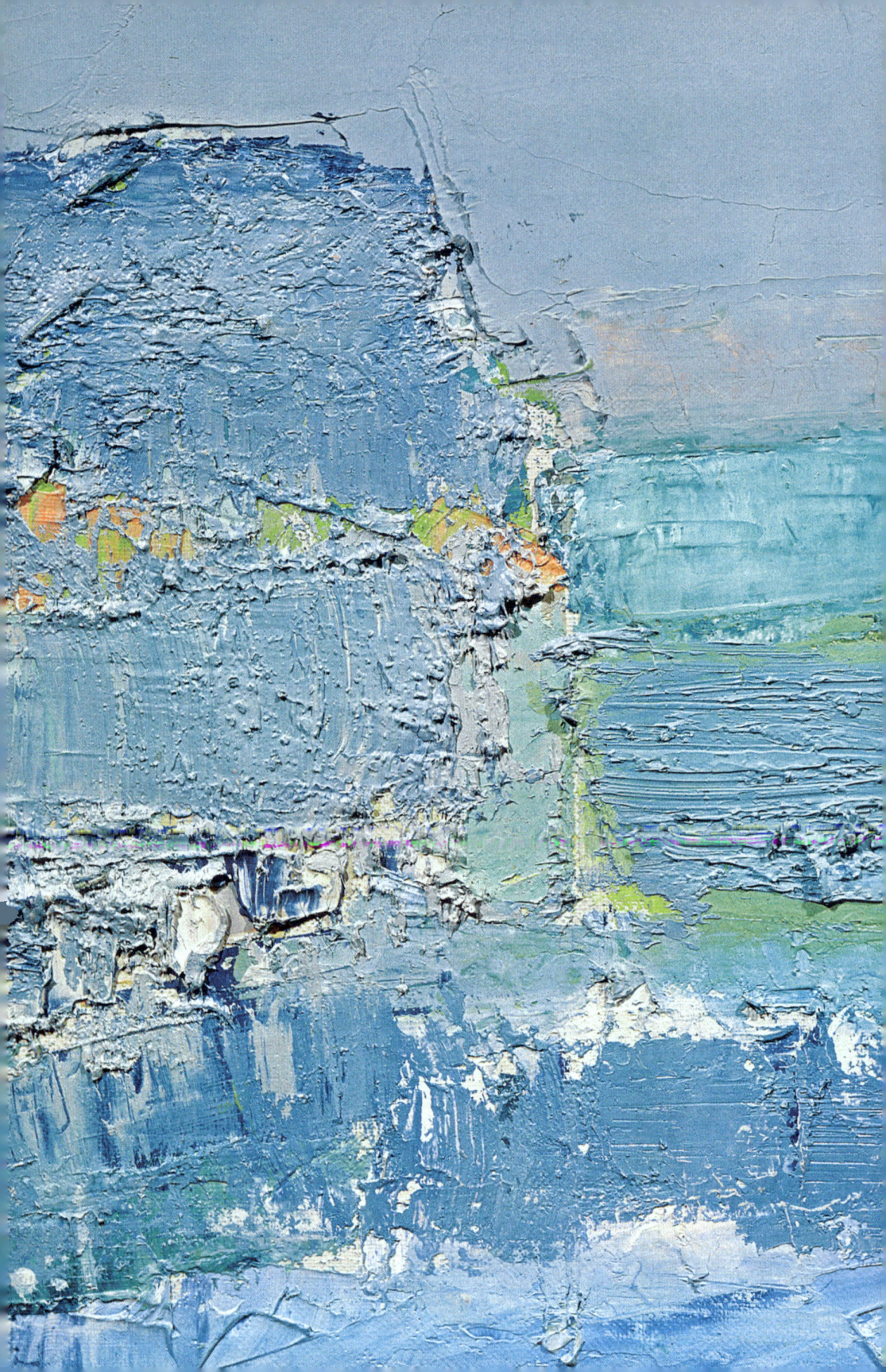

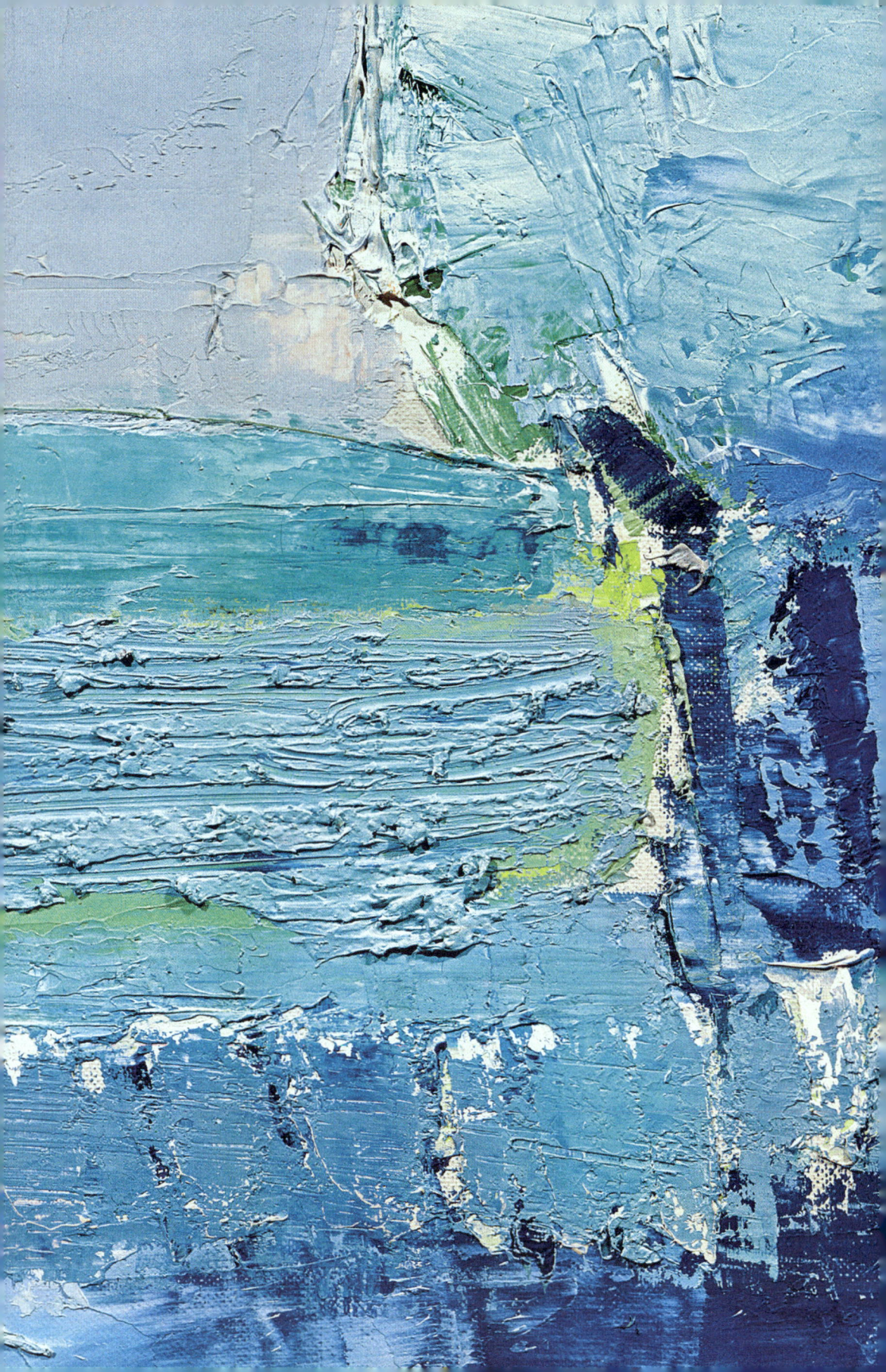

For All That We See or Seem

1967

A Blue Dream

One of the pioneers of the Narrative Figuration movement in France in the 1960s, Jacques Monory infused his daily life with his inner violence and anxieties.

How does one convey the neuroses of our world in everyday scenes? With a blue filter. In his paintings with their unmistakable blue (which he even sold under his name), Jacques Monory detached his subjects from the real world. He played on this ambiguous atmosphere in works oscillating between fantasy and anxiety. What better than the world of dreams in which to waver between reality and nightmare. The title he chose for this picture, from a poem by Edgar Allan Poe, tells us that 'all is but a dream within a dream'. Monory wrote: 'Behind the blue glass, I am protected from the bullets. For me blue is not the colour of fear. It is the colour of dreams'.

It is as if this colour is acting as a talisman, rendering the throes of existence less painful. Here Monory was representing a difficult period in his life: his separation from his partner. The man and the woman are isolated from one another, each with his car, as if about to take two separate routes, and above all separated by a white line like a fissure.

The blue filter is also a reference to the cinema that so inspired him. Here again it is a reference to a world of fantasy: everything always seems so much better in films. And there is also the distance that he liked to place between the real and the fictive. We always try to turn our dreams into reality but why not turn our reality into a dream?

Monory and the Cinema

Jacques Monory said that it was always the cinema that most inspired him, admitting that 'I was much more deeply moved by *Citizen Kane* than Veronese'. His paintings are full of references to films, ranging from *The Lady from Shanghai* to *Scarface* and *King Kong*.

TIMELINE
Blue in Films

1965 *Pierrot le Fou,* Jean-Luc Godard

Peau d'âne, Jacques Demy — **1970**

1988 *Le Grand bleu,* Luc Besson

Mulholland Drive, David Lynch — **2001**

2009 *Avatar,* James Cameron

Blue is the Warmest Colour, Abdellatif Kechiche — **2013**

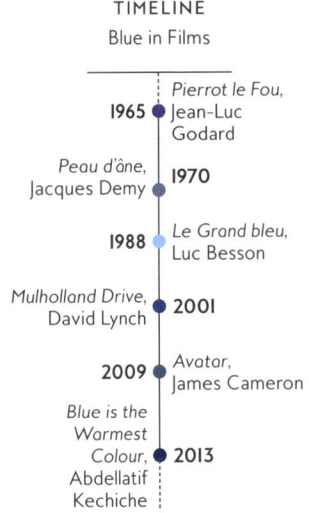

For All That We See or Seem, is a Dream Within a Dream
Jacques Monory (1924–2018)
1967
Oil on canvas
Musée d'Art contemporain, Marseille

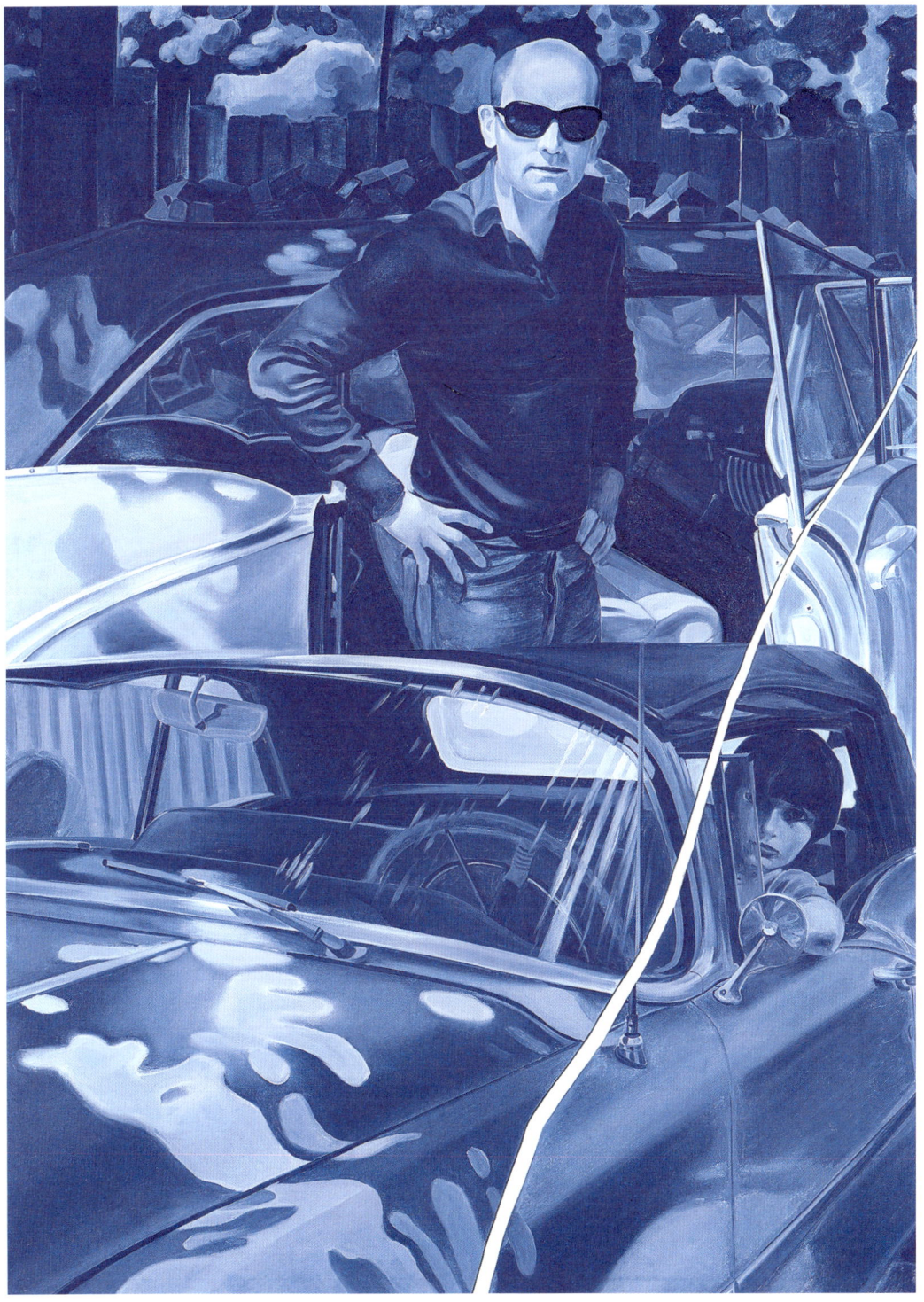

Untitled 1990

1990

Blue in India

For Hindus blue is the colour of the sky, symbol of the infinite, courage and truth. Many gods are portrayed with blue skin, Krishna and Vishnu for example. In Indian culture blue is also the colour of the weavers', artisans' and farmers' castes. Blue garments are forbidden for certain castes, the process of obtaining indigo dye being considered impure.

Fear of the Void

In the very late 1970s Anish Kapoor began using pure pigments referring to Holi, the Festival of Colours, in his native India.

He produced works clearly echoing the minimalism of American artists like Donald Judd. In 1985 he began a series of sculptures, titled *Void*, exploring the concepts of emptiness and the infinite. Their forms, convex or concave depending on the viewpoint, abolish the frontiers between air and the solid, while the velvety appearance of the pigments coating them gives them a sensual, tactile materiality.

Here the ovoid form is an allusion to the mother figure, whose blue robe, Kapoor explained, 'identifies her as a cosmic mother, an initiation'. It oscillates between the plenitude of a woman's rounded belly and the emptiness of her body after giving birth. Above all, this sculpture puts the viewer in an ambiguous position between attraction and repulsion that Freud would have appreciated. Is this both captive and disturbing 'mother' going to strike us?

By employing the intensity of ultramarine, Kapoor is referring to the immensity of the sky and the ocean and reinforcing the abyssal impression the work gives us. His blue hypnotises us, absorbs us, sucks us into it. And how it enjoys our fear of the unknown!

And yet if we look closer, the void the artist is playing with does not have the mean-spirited taste of emptiness. On the contrary, Kapoor's blue void is a promise of the infinite, a space where everything can be created.

Untitled 1990
Anish Kapoor (born 1954)
1990
Installation, fiberglass and pure pigment
Private collection

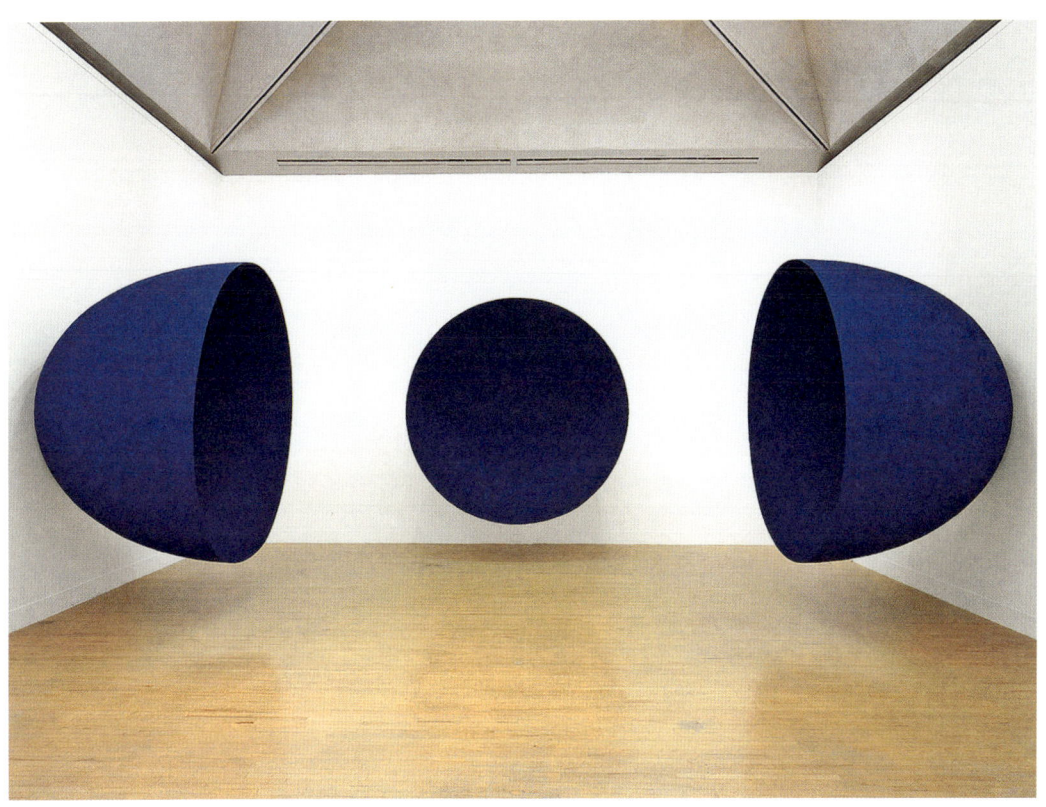

'I have conceived many works in black and in blue, because blue is a colour that reveals darkness much more. From a phenomenological point of view, our eyes cannot really concentrate on blue'.

Anish Kapoor

Untitled

1998

Losing One's Head

The Chinese artist Yue Minjun is known for his pictures peopled with caricatured figures with pink skin tones and cynical fits of laughter, whose irony he used against the political situation in his country.

Representing a fit of laughter cannot be censored, and this is exactly the weapon that Yue Minjun has used and abused to denounce the Chinese authorities. His laughs, like masks, devoid of emotion, accuse society and its absurdities.

And when the face and head disappear, the symbolism is even more powerful. With this figure, beheaded cleanly without a trace of blood, Yue Minjun adds a new dimension to his artistic attack - an absence.

His realistic style has not changed: the T-shirt and its folds are precisely painted and the musculature of the body is so realistically rendered that one is almost unsurprised by the absence of head. Yue Minjun has succeeded in drawing us into a comical universe in which the tragic has become banal in an allegory of present-day reality.

But the irony does not end there. With the uniform blue sky that could have been painted by David Hockney, the Chinese artist takes his sarcasm a step further. It is now this blue that seems to be cynically grinning at us. The dramatic is now comic, the absurd normal, suffering joy. Like an ostrich, the vanished head prefers to hide, but in the sky.

Irony that Denounces

Using humour to denounce or criticise has always been a redoubtable weapon: during the First World War the Dada movement broke with convention to ridicule society and its contradictions. Then Dada's direct heirs, the Surrealists, engaged in an idealistic political struggle, and much later Pop artists made fun of the symbols of consumer society

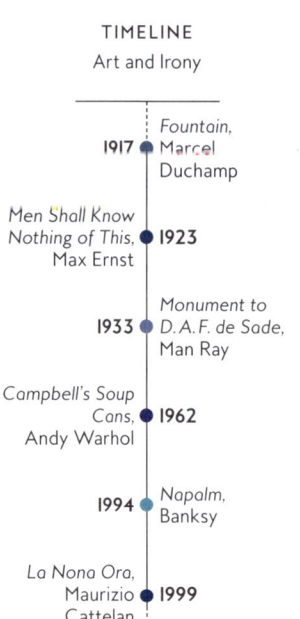

TIMELINE
Art and Irony

1917 — *Fountain,* Marcel Duchamp

Men Shall Know Nothing of This, Max Ernst — 1923

1933 — *Monument to D. A. F. de Sade,* Man Ray

Campbell's Soup Cans, Andy Warhol — 1962

1994 — *Napalm,* Banksy

La Nona Ora, Maurizio Cattelan — 1999

'No insults, much irony and gaiety:
insults revolt, irony forces people into themselves,
gaiety disarms'.

Voltaire

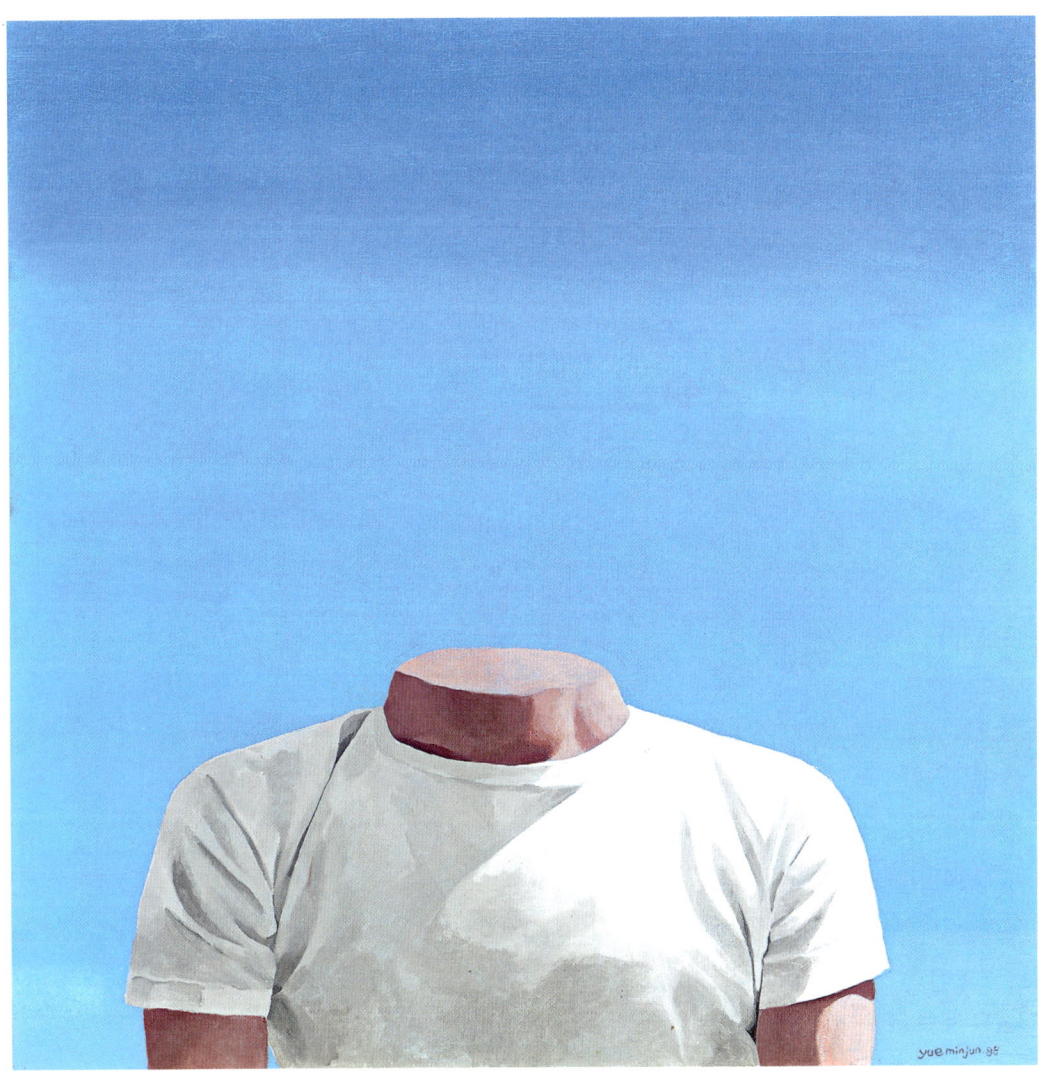

Untitled
Yue Minjun (born 1962)
1998
Oil on canvas
Private collection

List of Illustrations

THE
LESS EXPECTED

Page 63
The Ishtar Gate (detail)
ca. 580 BC.
Glazed bricks
Pergamonmuseum, Berlin

Page 65
Diana,
Ist century B.C. `
Fresco
Museo Archeologico Nationale, N
aples

Page 67
Mask of Xiuhtecuhtli
1400-1521
Wood, mother-of pearl and
turquoise mosaic
16 × 13 cm
British Museum, London

Page 69
The Drapers' Window
ca. 1460
Stained glass
Collegiate Church of Notre-Dame,
Semur-en-Auxois

Pages 71 and 5 (detail)
Wall tile
1525-50
Iznik ceramic with underglaze
decoration
30.5 × 25.1cm
Victoria and Albert Museum, London

Page 73
The Opening of the Fifth Seal,
El Greco
1614
Oil on canvas
224.8 × 199.4cm
The Metropolitan Museum of Art,
New York

Pages 75 and 3 (detail)
Marie-Henriette Berthelot de
Pléneuf,
Jean-Marc Nattier
1739
Oil on canvas
101.8 × 82.8cm
Musée de l'Art occidental, Tokyo

Pages 77 and 78/79 (detail)
The Monk by the Sea,
Caspar David Friedrich
1808-10
Oil on canvas
110 × 171.5cm
Alte Nationalgalerie, Berlin

Page 81
Nocturne in Blue and Silver:
Chelsea,
James McNeill Whistler
1871
Oil on wood
50.2 × 60.8cm
Tate Collection, London

Page 83
The Golden Cell,
Odilon Redon
1892
Pastel and oil on paper
31 × 24.7cm
British Museum, London

Page 85
Manhattan Bridge,
Eugene de Salignac
1922
Cyanotype
19.1 × 22.9cm
Worcester Art Museum, Worcester

Pages 87 and 88/89 (detail)
Street Decked in American
Banners,
Raoul Dufy
ca. 1930
Oil on cardboard
44.5 × 54.6cm
Private collection

Page 91
Sky Blue,
Wassily Kandinsky
1940
Oil on canvas
100 × 73cm
Musée national d'Art moderne,
Centre Pompidou, Paris

Pages 93 and 60/61 (detail)
Sea Watchers,
Edward Hopper
1952
Oil on canvas
76.2 × 10.6cm
Private collection

Pages 95 and 96/97 (detail)
Provence Landcape,
Nicolas de Staël
1953
Oil on canvas
33 × 46cm
Museo Thyssen-Bornemisza, Madrid

Page 99
For All That We See or Seem,
Jacques Monory
1967
Oil on canvas
Musée d'Art contemporain, Marseille

Page 101
Untitled 1990,
Anish Kapoor
1990
Installation, fiberglass and pigment
205 × 205 × 230cm
Private collection

Page 103
Untitled,
Yue Minjun
1998
Oil on canvas
69.9 × 69.9cm
Private collection

PHOTOGRAPHIC CREDITS

© Adagp, Paris, 2019 / Photo: Lefevre Fine Art Ltd., London / Bridgeman Images: 60/61, 93.
© Adagp, Paris, 2019 / Photo: Christie's / Bridgeman Images: 87, 88/89.
© Adagp, Paris, 2019 / Photo: Thyssen-Bornemisza Collection, Madrid, Spain / Bridgeman Images: 95, 96/97.
© Adagp, Paris, 2019 / Photo: Ville de Marseille, Dist. RMN-Grand Palais / Benjamin Soligny / Raphaël Chipault: 99.
© Agnew's, London / Bridgeman Images: 3, 75.
© Alte Nationalgalerie, Berlin / Bridgeman Images: 77, 78/79.
© Anish Kapoor. All Rights Reserved, DACS / Adagp, Paris, 2019: 101.
© BnF, Dist. RMN-Grand Palais / image BnF: 27.
© Christie's Images / Bridgeman Images: 35.
© Notre-Dame, Semur-en-Auxois, France / Bridgeman Images: 69.
© David Hockney / Tate, London, 2019: 59.
© Metropolitan Museum of Art, New York, USA / Bridgeman Images: 14/15, 17, 37, 73.

© Musée d'Orsay, Paris, France / Bridgeman Images: 2, 39.
© Musée national d'Art moderne, Centre Pompidou, Paris, France / Peter Willi / Bridgeman Images: 91.
© Museo Archeologico Nazionale, Naples, Italy / Index Fototeca / Bridgeman Images: 65.
© Natural History Museum, London, UK / Bridgeman Images: 9.
© Pergamonmuseum, Berlin / Tarker / Bridgeman Images: 63.
© Priscilla Mason and William Grimm Funds / Bridgeman Images: 85.
© Rijksmuseum, Amsterdam, The Netherlands / Bridgeman Images: 31.
© RMN-Grand Palais (Domaine de Chantilly) / René-Gabriel Ojéda: 25.
© RMN-Grand Palais (Musée Adrien Dubouché) / Tony Querrec: 33.
© RMN-Grand Palais (MNAAG, Paris) / Thierry Ollivier: 23.
© RMN-Grand Palais (Orsay) / Hervé Lewandowski: 49, 50/51.
© RMN-Grand Palais (Louvre) / Stéphane Maréchalle: 4, 29.
© Scrovegni Chapel, Padua, Italy / Cameraphoto Arte Venezia / Bridgeman Images: 19, 20/21.

© Städtische Galerie im Lenbachhaus, Munich, Germany / Artothek / Bridgeman Images: 47.
© Successió Miró / Adagp, Paris, 2019 / Photo: Pierre Matisse Gallery, New York, USA / Bridgeman Images: 53.
© Succession Matisse / Photo: Musée national d'Art moderne, Centre Pompidou, Paris, France / Peter Willi / Bridgeman Images: 55.
© Succession Picasso 2019 / Photo: RMN-Grand Palais (Musée national Picasso-Paris) / Mathieu Rabeau: 45.
© Succession Yves Klein c/o Adagp, Paris, 2019 / Photo: Philippe Migeat - Centre Pompidou, MNAM-CCI / Dist. RMN-GP: 57.
© Tate, London, Dist. RMN-Grand Palais / Tate Photography: 81, 106/7.
© The British Museum, London, Dist. RMN-Grand Palais / Trustees of the British Museum: 67, 83.
© The National Gallery, London, Dist. RMN-Grand Palais / National Gallery: 41, 42/43.
© Victoria and Albert Museum, London, Dist. RMN-Grand Palais / image V&A Museum: 5, 71.
© Yue Minjun / Photo: Christie's Images / Bridgeman: 103.

Impressum

First published in French by © Hachette Livre (Éditions du Chêne), 2019
Original title: Bleu. De L'égypte ancienne à Yves Klein

© Prestel Verlag, Munich · London · New York 2026
A member of Penguin Random House Verlagsgruppe GmbH
Neumarkter Strasse 28 · 81673 Munich

1st edition 2026

produktsicherheit@penguin-randomhouse.de
(The above information is mandatory information according to GPSR and should be used for all queries relating to the safety of our books)

The publisher expressly reserves the right to exploit the copyrighted content of this work for the purposes of text and data mining in accordance with Section 44b of the German Copyright Act (UrhG), based on the European Digital Single Market Directive. Any unauthorized use is an infringement of copyright and is hereby prohibited.

A CIP catalogue record for this book is available from the British Library.
Library of Congress Control Number: 2025946060

Éditions du Chêne:
Director: Emmanuel Le Vallois
Edition: Hélène Sevin
Art director: Sabine Houplain
Graphic design: Sophie Della Corte
French proofreaders: Clémentine Bougrat, Valérie Mettais
Production: Marc Chalmin
Separations: Hyphen Group, Orio al Serio, Italy

Translation: David Wharry
Copyediting: Russell Stockman
Editorial direction Prestel: Markus Eisen
Production management: Martina Effaga
Typesetting: Uhl+Massopust GmbH
Printing and binding: M Paper, Huizhou, China

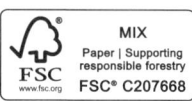

Penguin Random House Verlagsgruppe FSC® N001967

Printed in China

ISBN 978-3-7913-9429-9

www.prestel.com